Card Tricks
for Beginners

Wilfrid Jonson

Edited by
Chesley V. Barnes

Dover Publications, Inc.
Mineola, New York

Bibliographical Note

This Dover edition, first published in 2004, is an unabridged republication of *Card Conjuring,* originally published by W. & G. Foyle, Ltd., London, in 1950 and republished by Dover Publications, Inc., New York, in 1954 as part of the volume *Magic Tricks & Card Tricks.*

Library of Congress Cataloging-in-Publication Data

Jonson, Wilfrid.
   Card tricks for beginners / Wilfrid Jonson ; edited by Chesley V. Barnes.
      p. cm.
   Rev. ed. of: Card tricks. c1954.
   Includes bibliographical references and index.
   ISBN-13: 978-0-486-43465-0 (pbk.)
   ISBN-10: 0-486-43465-6 (pbk.)
      1. Card tricks. I. Barnes, Chesley V. II. Jonson, Wilfrid. Card tricks.
III. Title.

GV1549.J47 2004
793.8'5—dc22

2003063496

Manufactured in the United States by LSC Communications
43465611   2018
www.doverpublications.com

CONTENTS

PART I

PART II

CONTENTS—*continued*

PREFACE

THE scope of this book is very similar to that of its companion volume *A Handbook of Conjuring* and, while an acquaintance with that work is not essential, its perusal is recommended, since, although the technique of conjuring with cards is very different from that of ordinary conjuring, the principles of its presentation remain the same. This Handbook, like its companion, aims at illustrating those principles with a representtive selection of tricks which the amateur can perform without an excessive amount of practice, and will not require the reader to spend weary hours in the pursuit of excessive dexterity.

We would impress upon the reader the plain fact that the first aim of the conjurer is to entertain. If he will always remember that fact he will not go far wrong. For our part we shall refrain from including in this handbook any tricks which, however mystifying they may be, are boring, such as those in which the pack is four times dealt into thirteen heaps, and similar rigmaroles sometimes dear to compilers of books on card conjuring.

While pure dexterity with cards can, in the hands of a master, produce astonishing results, the majority of card tricks are effected by subtlety and misdirection more than by skill. The tricks themselves are often very simple and the art of the conjurer lies in dressing them up so that they appear to be miraculous. The beginner usually pays too little attention to this part of his business : neglects the dressing and spoils the trick. We shall clothe each trick in an appropriate costume and ask you to notice the skill with which the costume conceals the trick's weak points ; how the dressing distracts the spectator's mind from the fallacy which he must not be allowed to perceive.

LONDON, 1950   WILFRID JONSON

PART 1

THE Author of the Ingoldsby Legends was neither the first
nor the last gentleman of the cloth to betray an astonishing
knowledge of card conjuring. To have " an Ace or a King at
the bottom " or, indeed to have any *known* card there, is a
great advantage to a card conjurer, as our first trick will show.

" THAT'S IT "

With a card that you know upon the bottom of the pack,
you put it down upon the table and ask a spectator to cut it
into two parts. Invite him to take a card from either portion
and to show it to the company, without letting you see what
card it is. When the card has been shown to all, ask the
chooser to replace it upon either portion and note carefully
upon which heap he does replace it, but do not let your
interest in this point be apparent to the spectators.

If he replaces the card upon the portion that was previously
the uppermost part of the pack, tell him to drop the other
portion on top of it. Let him then cut the pack and complete
the cut in card playing fashion.

But should he replace the card upon the other packet, the
original bottom part of the pack, ask him to cut that portion
and complete the cut, thus burying the selected card in that
packet, to put the two halves of the pack together and to cut
once more.

Perhaps we had better clarify this business of cutting for
the benefit of any readers unacquainted with card playing
practice. In games of cards the person who shuffles the pack
places it upon the table before a second player who cuts by
lifting off a portion of the cards and putting them down on the
table by the side of the remainder of the pack. The dealer
then *completes the cut* by picking up the original lower portion

9

and placing it upon the other. So, when these actions are combined by one person, to *cut and complete the cut* one lifts off a portion of the pack and puts it down on the table. One then picks up the remainder of the cards and puts them on top of the other portion. Cutting the pack is often regarded as the great safeguard of the honest player against the crooked gambler, and many card players display a faith in the virtues of cutting which is not borne out by the facts, as will presently be clear to you.

But to return to our trick. Whichever of the two procedures outlined above has been followed, the practical result is the same, the original bottom card of the pack has been placed immediately above the selected card.

You now take the pack and turning it face upwards, spread it from left to right in a long overlapping row, so that the indices of all the cards can easily be seen. With a little practice you will find that, with a good clean pack of cards, you can do this with one swift and skilful sweep of the hand. Now you hold your forefinger an inch or two above the cards and say to the chooser of the card : " I will pass my finger slowly along the cards like this. When it passes above your card I want you to think to yourself 'That's it.' Do not say anything, do not move a muscle, but every time my finger passes over your card simply think to yourself, ' That's it.' "

You pass your finger slowly along the row of cards from one end to the other and you look for the card you know, the original bottom one. The chosen card is the one below it, the one to its right in the row of cards. You do not pause when you reach it but carry on to the end of the row and say : " I did not get it that time. Again please." You carry your finger back along the row and a little way past the selected card ; then you pause and let your hand, with its pointing finger, swing in pendulum fashion, above the section of the row of cards in which the selected one lies. Then in a hesitant fashion you lower your finger and let it fall upon the chosen card.

In card conjuring one can often do more by intelligent planning and anticipation than by much sleight-of-hand and it would be a great pity if, at the conclusion of the preceding trick, one failed to take advantage of the fact that the cards are all spread out before you. So, before you gather them up you will remember the third and fourth cards from the bottom, that is from the right hand end of the overlapping row. Then you slip one finger beneath the top card, the card at the left hand end, and neatly gather up the overlapping row of the cards with one quick sweep of the hand. Much of the charm of good conjuring lies in the precision and dexterity with which the performer handles the cards and even such a simple action as gathering up the spread out pack can be done with elegance and distinction.

A MATHEMATICAL CERTAINTY

Knowing the names of the third and fourth cards from the bottom you put the pack down upon the table and ask one of the spectators to cut it into two heaps. When he has done so you ask him to touch one of the heaps. And here we come to an artifice often used in conjuring . . . . to apparently give a spectator a free choice when, in reality, whatever he may say the trick will take the same, premeditated, course. If the spectator touches the original bottom half of the pack you ask him to pick up that half, while you yourself pick up the other half. But if he touches the original top half you pick that up yourself, saying, " Very good. Will you take the other half then." Notice that you do not ask him to *choose* one of the heaps but simply ask him to *touch* one of them.

You now ask the spectator to " do everything that I do. Will you count your cards first." You count by dealing the cards one by one on to the table. The spectator does the same and as counting in this manner reverses the order of the cards, the two cards that you know were previously the third and fourth from the bottom will now be the third and fourth from the top of his heap of cards. Announce the number of cards in your heap and ask how many he has. Behave as if the matter was important. Actually it has nothing whatever to do with the trick but it is valuable " misdirection." Whatever number he announces ask him to discard one card. He will naturally discard the top one.

Ask him next to continue doing exactly as you do. Take the top card of your heap and slip it into the centre. Wait while he does the same. Take a card from the bottom and put it into the centre. Take a second card from the top and place it in your right coat pocket. Take another from the bottom and put it in the centre of the cards you hold. Take one more card from the top and put it into your left coat pocket. Put your cards down on the table. If the assisting spectator follows all these actions, which have been deliberately designed to drag so many red herrings across the trail, the card in his right-hand coat pocket is the one that was originally the third from the bottom of the pack and the card in his left-hand coat pocket is that which was originally fourth from the bottom.

You bring the trick to a climax by saying, " It is a mathematical certainty that this card in my left-hand pocket being the . . . ." (you bring it out and name it as you show it) " the card in your right-hand pocket is the . . . ." (you name the first of the two cards you have remembered) " and this one being the . . . . " (you take the card from your right-hand pocket and name it also) "the one in your other pocket is the . . . " (You name the second card you have remembered.) " Am I right, sir ? "

FALSE SHUFFLING I

If it is useful to know the card on the bottom of the pack, it is still more useful to be able to shuffle the cards and yet keep it there. It is not a difficult thing to do, in fact it is quite the simplest form of False Shuffle. But first we had better make sure that you know how to shuffle a pack of cards, for many people do not.

A good shuffle is one that mixes the cards thoroughly and leaves them so that neither the shuffler nor any spectator knows even the approximate position of a single card. We will confess at once that a really good shuffle is very rarely made but we will tell you how you may make a fairly good one. Take the pack in your left hand, face downwards, its left edge resting on the palm of your hand, the bottom card lying against your fingers and your thumb lying upon the top card of the pack. Grasp the pack by its ends with the right hand, the fingers at the far end of the pack and the thumb at the near end, and lift up all but a few of the top cards, which you retain in the left hand by a slight pressure of the left thumb. As the right hand raises the bulk of the pack the cards remaining in the left hand fall face down upon the left fingers. The right hand returns with the balance of the pack and a few more cards are deposited upon those in the left hand, being half dropped and half pulled off by the left thumb. The process is repeated until the whole of the pack has been returned to the left hand in little instalments. That is the true shuffle.

Let us ask you to remember two technical terms which will facilitate future description, for conjuring also has its technical jargon. The action of drawing away the underpart of the pack is called an " under-cut." The action of shuffling the cards in the right hand on to those in the left is called " shuffling off."

To false shuffle without disturbing the bottom card you first undercut three quarters or more of the pack but, as you do so, your left finger tips press against the face of the bottom card and keep it in position so that it remains in the left hand beneath the top cards. The balance of the pack is then shuffled off and the bottom card will have remained unchanged.

THE SEVEN HEAPS.

Having secretly noted the bottom card of the pack you false shuffle the cards to leave the bottom one undisturbed and put the pack, face down, upon the table. You ask a spectator to divide the pack into seven heaps, and you remember the position of the heap with your noted card at the bottom. Such a known card, by the way, is called a " key card " and we shall thus refer to it in the future.

You ask the spectator to remove any card from any of the seven heaps, to remember it, to show it to the other spectators, and then to drop it on the top of any heap. That done you gather the heaps together again, apparently haphazardly, but actually you take care to drop the heap with the key card on top of the chosen card, and to leave the chosen card somewhere near the centre of the reassembled pack. You should handle the heaps neatly and carelessly ; neatly so that you may not be suspected of any sleight-of-hand, carelessly so that the fact that you keep track of the position of the card will not be observed. Pick up each heap by its ends between the second finger and the thumb and drop each one daintily upon the next. Ask the spectator now to cut the pack and to complete the cut, and observe the depth of his cut. If he cuts deep, that is to say, if he lifts up more than half the cards, the selected card will be left somewhere near the bottom of the pack, while if he cuts high the card will be towards the top.

Take the pack and, holding it face upwards, casually spread the cards between your hands. Look for the original bottom card (the key card) and quickly notice the name of the card below it, to the right of the key card in the face up pack. This is the selected card and since you know its approximate position in the pack, you should need only a quick glance at the cards to find it. Close the pack and shuffle it casually. Let us suppose the chosen card is the six of spades. Take any club and any red card from the pack and place them face up upon the table. Ask the spectator to fix his mind very strongly upon the colour of his card. Pause for a moment and then, since the selected card is a spade, pick up the red card and put it back in the pack and take a spade from the pack and put it down beside the club. Ask the spectator to think then of the suit of his card. After a moment's hesitation return the club to the pack. Turn the pack face downwards and begin to deal cards very slowly on to the table, counting aloud and saying

" Ace, two, three, four, five, six . . . . You are thinking of the six of Spades. Is that right ? "

Notice the dressing please. To the spectators the trick will appear less like a card trick than like an experiment in thought reading.

FALSE SHUFFLING II

It is sometimes more useful to know the top card than the bottom one and when that is so the simplest method, very often, is to secretly glance at the bottom card and then to shuffle it to the top. This is very easily done by undercutting about three quarters of the pack and shuffling off until only a few cards remain in the right hand. The cards are held in the right hand between the thumb and the second finger, and you will find it a simple matter, at this point, to slightly straighten finger and thumb so as to hold only the bottom card and let all the others fall on to the pack. The last card is then dropped on top.

We hope that you are trying all these things as you come to them. You will make no progress in card conjuring by reading this book and sitting back and thinking about it. You must take the cards in your hands and try the actions as we describe them. Although we shall not ask you to learn anything very difficult even the simplest piece of conjuring technique requires a certain amount of practice.

We hardly think it should be necessary for us to explain how one may shuffle the top card of the pack to the bottom, but for the sake of completeness we will describe the simple procedure.

Commence the shuffle by drawing off the top card with the left thumb and then shuffle off the remainder of the pack. It is as well to immediately shuffle the pack again, keeping the card in its place on the bottom.

You should notice that by combining these two shuffles you may take the top card of the pack to the bottom at the same time that you shuffle the bottom one to the top.

THE CHANGING CARD

Secretly notice the bottom card of the pack, shuffle it to the top and hand the pack to one of the spectators. Ask him to think of a number. Tell him he may choose any number he wishes but that, to save time, you would suggest a number under twenty. When he has decided upon his number, turn your back and ask him to deal on to the table the number of cards he thought of; quietly, so that you will not be able to hear the cards fall. Ask him then to turn up the top card of those in his hand, to remember it and to show it to the other spectators, to replace it, to replace the cards he dealt, to cut the pack, and to complete the cut.

When he has done all this (the effect of which is to place your key card above his chosen card) you take the pack from him and holding it so that the spectators cannot see the faces of the cards, you spread it in a fan and find the key card. The one to the right of it will be the selected one. Let us suppose the selected card is the eight of Clubs. Draw the next card to the right, which we will suppose is the two of Hearts, over the eight of Clubs so as to conceal it and spread the cards a little so that the two cards, lined up as one, are a little free from the rest of the fanned pack. Hold the fan in the left hand and lower it so that the faces may now be seen by the spectators. Grasp the two cards between the right hand first finger and thumb and say : " Your card was not the two of Hearts, was it?" (naming the visible card). Raise the fan again so that the backs of the cards are towards the spectators and, as you do so, draw out the rear card of the two, the selected eight of Clubs and place it face down on the table. To the spectators it will appear that you have put the two of Hearts upon the table. Cut the pack to leave the two on the top.

Spread the pack in a fan again and remove another card *in exactly the same way as you did the first*, that is, show it in the fan, name it, and remove it as you turn the back of the fan to the spectators. Put this card, which we will suppose is he four of Diamonds, on the table beside the first.

Ask the assisting spectator to touch "one of the cards, the two of Hearts or the four of Diamonds." If he touches the four, turn it over and return it to the pack, then ask him to put his hand upon the other card and hold it tightly. If he touches the eight of Clubs, however, the supposed two of Hearts, tell him to keep his finger firmly upon it, turn up the four of Diamonds and return it to the centre of the pack. The " choice " is forced and in either case the spectator keeps his hand upon the chosen card while he believes he has the two of Hearts.

Ask the name of the selected card and say you will make it change places with the two. Ruffle the pack, that is to say, holding it in the left hand with the thumb across its back, lift up the ends of the cards with the right second finger tip and then release them so that they make a rustling, crackling noise. Then turn over the top card of the pack . . . .the two of Hearts !

Ask the spectator to turn up the card beneath his hand . . . . it is the selected one !

FALSE SHUFFLING III

We shall now ask you to learn a kind of false shuffling which is rather more complicated but which you should be able to acquire without difficulty thanks to your practising of the simpler kinds. We will call it the Pick Up Shuffle. It can be used for a variety of purposes but we will describe it first as it is used to retain a number of cards undisturbed upon the top of the pack, in other words a false shuffle to retain the top stock.

Commence the shuffle by under-cutting the pack, as we have already described, leaving the top cards which you desire to retain (the top stock) and a few more in the left hand. The bulk of the pack, in the right hand, should be held solely by the second finger and thumb, leaving the other fingers, and particularly the third one free. Bring the right hand down to the left so that the cards it holds cover the top stock and, beneath them, grasp the top stock with the right third finger against the right thumb. Leave a good packet of cards in the left

hand and lift the right, carrying the top stock away hidden
beneath the rest of the cards. Shuffle these cards off until the
stock is reached and then drop that on top.

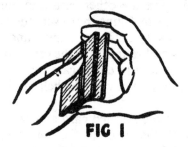

FIG I

Figure 1 shows the position as the right hand moves upwards carrying away the top stock concealed beneath the other
cards. The stock is held between the third finger and the
thumb, and the other cards are held by the second finger and
the thumb. The illustration, of course, shows the position
as you see it yourself. The hands should be held so that the
spectators see only the backs of the cards.

The shuffle is not difficult to do but you must practise it
until you can do it practically without thinking about it and
can pick up the top stock beneath the other cards without the
slightest hesitation.

THE SENSE OF TOUCH

It is very convenient to give every trick a name by which
it may be remembered, but the fabrication of titles is not
always easy.

To be able to shuffle a pack and leave certain cards undisturbed on the top is of little value without a way of finding
out what those cards are, or of secretly putting certain known
cards in place. Many books on conjuring blithely ignore this
difficulty and leave the beginner to solve the problem by himself. He sometimes solves it, as we have seen an amateur do, by
using a different pack for every trick, each one having been
arranged beforehand ! We shall teach you a trick now which
will give you the opportunity to find a few cards and to put

them on the top of the pack. The cards we shall seek are an ace, a two, a four, and an eight, all of different suits, which we shall need for the following trick. To prepare for one trick in the course of another is a very useful stratagem. The trick we give you will also teach you another method of using the known card upon the bottom of the pack.

Begin by glancing at the bottom card and remembering it ; then shuffle the pack without disturbing that card. Spread the pack between your hands, in a wide fan, as neatly as possible, and ask a spectator to choose one. When he has drawn a card, ask him to show it to the rest of the audience without letting you see it. Unless there is some good reason to the contrary it is always wise to have this done. Without this precaution you are at the mercy of a single person, who may forget the card he drew or even maliciously deny it. While the card is being shown close the pack, cut it and complete the cut, bringing your key card, your known card, to the centre, but hold a little division in the pack by inserting the tip of your little finger beneath the key card as shown in Figure 2. Such a division in the pack is called a " break ".

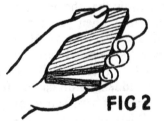

FIG 2

You now ask the selector to replace his card in the pack and you cut the cards and hold out the bottom half towards him. He replaces his card upon it and you drop the other half of the pack on top. But you have cut, of course, at the break held by your little finger tip, and so, the selected card is beneath your key card. You now shuffle the pack, taking care not to separate the two cards, by drawing off a fairly large packet of cards when you approach the middle of the pack where the two cards lie.

You now state that you have a very remarkable sense of touch, sensitive to even the slightest vibrations of thought. You ask the selector of the card to keep his mind upon its identity while you deal the cards upon the table.

You push the top card half way off the pack with your left thumb and run your right fingers over its face as though you were feeling its pips. You turn the card so that all may see it and then deal it face down upon the table. Without seeming to do so you glance at the face of the card yourself. A little experimenting will show you just how much the cards must be turned for you to be able to see the faces without the fact being obvious to the spectators. You continue dealing the cards one by one like this, quickly feeling the face of each one and throwing them haphazardly down on the table, and you watch for your key card. You also watch for the four cards you require, an Ace, a two, a four, and an eight of different suits, and as you come to these you deal them a little to one side so that presently you will be able to gather them up separately from the rest of the pack.

You should have found your four cards by the time the key card appears. You know that the next card is the selected one and you must not pause when you reach it but show it and deal it face down like the others. However, you carefully notice exactly where the selected card falls and you mark it by dealing another card on to its back. You deal a few more cards and then you suddenly stop as you feel the face of the next one. With a smile of satisfaction on your face you say to the spectators : " My remarkable sense of touch tells me that the next card to turn up is the selected one." Then you stop, as if bewildered by the expressions of incredulity shown by the spectators, all of whom have already seen the selected card dealt on to the table. You finger the card on top of those that remain and repeat : " Yes, the next card I turn up will be yours." The way in which this is received will depend a good deal upon the manners and breeding of your audience and upon the degree of intimacy between you, but people have been found rash enough at times to bet that the next card is

not the selected one. In which case you repeat your state-
ment : " The next card I turn up will be yours " and *turn up
the selected card on the table.*

During the ensuing laughter you gather up the cards,
quietly putting your Ace, two, four, and eight on the top of
the pack, *in that order.*

THE MATCHING CARDS

With your Ace, two, four, and eight upon the top of your
pack you execute the Pick Up Shuffle to leave them undisturbed
and, placing the pack upon the table, you ask a spectator to
cut it into two portions. When he has done so you pick up
the original top half and invite him to take the other. You
ask him to shuffle his cards and you do the same with yours.
Actually you false shuffle yours by first shuffling off four cards,
one by one, and then shuffling the rest on top of them. This
is a very convincing form of false shuffle but its only result is
to transfer your four top cards to the bottom of your half pack.

You now place your cards in your right coat pocket and
invite the spectator to do the same with his, and you announce a further demonstraton of your remarkable sense of
touch. For once you may tell your audience what you are
going to do before you have done it, although, as we explained
in the Handbook of Conjuring this is not, as a general rule,
a wise thing to do. You state that you will ask the assisting
spectator to draw a card from his pocket, haphazard, and by
sense of touch alone you will draw cards that match it from
your pocket. And this you do.

Let us suppose that your four cards, which are now on the
bottom of the half pack in your pocket, are the Ace of Clubs,
two of Diamonds, four of Hearts, and eight of Spades. The
spectator draws from his pocket the ten of Clubs. You draw
from your pocket the bottom card, the Ace of Clubs, saying
" This matches the suit." Then you withdraw the second card,
the two, leave the third, and bring out the eight, saying :
" And these two give the value." It is best not to look at the

cards but to run the finger tips across their faces to sustain the fiction that the sense of touch is alone responsible.

As another example : if the assistant drew the Ace of Spades you would draw the first and fourth cards from the bottom of your half pack, an Ace and a Spade.

For the three of Hearts you would produce your Ace, your two, and your Heart.

Counting Jacks as eleven, Queens as twelve, and Kings as thirteen, all the cards in the pack can be matched by your Ace, two, four, and eight.

THE PICK UP CONTROL

The theme of a very large number of card tricks is that spectators draw cards from the pack, remember them, and replace them. The conjurer then finds the cards in some ingenious way.

To do this the conjurer has to control the selected card in some unsuspected manner so that while it appears to be lost in the pack it is really kept in a known position, generally on the top of the pack. The old books from which we learnt the business, so many years ago, had practically only one method of control, the Two Handed Pass, which is really a secret cut. It is an excellent method, and we use it ourselves, but, unfortunately, it is so difficult that several years of patient practising must be spent to acquire any mastery of it, and a life-time may be passed in a vain effort to perfect it. Fortunately other methods have been invented during the last fifty years, years which have seen a revolution in the technique of card conjuring, and one of the best of these methods uses the Pick Up Shuffle which we have just taught you.

You spread the cards between your hands in a wide open fan and invite a spectator to choose one. When he has shown it to the rest of the company you invite him to return it to the pack, which you begin to shuffle from the right hand into the left. You pause in your shuffle and extend your left hand towards him and, quite naturally, he replaces his card upon the others in that hand. Apparently you at once shuffle the rest of the pack on top of the chosen card but actually, when the right hand comes down with its packet, you pick up a few cards, including the selected one, beneath it, and carry them away with the cards in the right hand. You then complete the shuffle and leave the selected card on the top of the pack.

THE CARD AND THE NUMBER

One of the most effective ways of revealing a selected card which has been " lost " in the pack is to find it at a numerical position chosen by a member of the audience. We shall give you a simple and amusing method.

Let a spectator choose a card, show it to the company, and replace it as you shuffle the pack. Bring the card to the top of the pack by means of the Pick Up Shuffle and then tell the chooser of it that you will invest him with your powers for a moment and enable him to find his card himself. Ask one of the other spectators to give you a number and suggest a number under twenty to save time. Let us assume that twelve is chosen. Hand the pack to the selector and instruct him to hold it in his left hand, to snap his fingers above it, and to order his card to fly to the twelfth place in the pack. When he does this (he will generally be rather sheepish about it) shake your head and say " Oh no, not like that ! "

Take the pack from him saying, " You won't get any results like that. You were not concentrating." Quickly count off eleven cards, by dealing on to the table, and turn up the twelfth, asking if it is the selected one. It is not. Replace all the cards on top of the pack and the selected card, originally on top, will now be the twelfth from the top.

Hand the pack to the spectator and ask him to try again. Tell him he must concentrate upon the job and do it with confidence. Ask the second spectator what number he chose, as though you had forgotten it, and get the selector to name his card and order it to fly to the chosen position.

Let him count down for himself and find it.

THE CORNER CRIMP

He would be a rather poor and ill-equipped conjurer who always used the same method to control a selected card, and we will now introduce you to another method which is very simple but, if properly used, very effective. You simply bend the inner right hand corner of the bottom card of the pack and use that card as a key card. Such a bend in a card is called a *crimp*. The corner crimp is easily made by placing the first finger tip underneath the corner and pulling down with the second finger tip as shown in Figure 3. Of course

FIG 3

the right hand rests above the pack, its thumb at the inner end and its fingers at the far end, and hides the left hand while it makes the crimp. In the illustration we have shown the left hand alone to make the action quite clear. The crimp should not be made too strongly. There is no need to break the corner of the card and the more expert you become in its use the less you will need to bend the corner.

You may crimp your card either before you start your trick or while the chooser of the card is showing it to the other spectators, but in either case you then cut the pack to bring the crimped card to the centre. When you ask the chooser to replace his card you have the pack lying face down in your left hand and you lift up half the pack with your right. In doing so your right thumb finds the slight break in the pack made by the crimped card and cuts the pack at that point. The selector replaces his card and you drop the half pack fairly on top and deliberately square the cards.

You pause for a moment and make some remarks regarding your trick and then you cut the pack again, once more cutting at the crimped card and bringing the selected one to the top of the pack. Immediately you false shuffle the pack, first shuffling the selected card to the bottom and then shuffling it back to the top.

Practise cutting at a crimped card, in the manner we have described, until you can find it at once, without hesitation, by the sense of touch alone. You must not look at the cards when you do this.

THE REVERSED CARD

An excellent way of revealing the selected card after you have brought it to the top of the pack is to find it turned face upward, and this may be done readily in the following amusing fashion.

With the pack in the left hand in the position for dealing, and the selected card on top of it, you pull out the bottom card and, showing it, ask if it is the chosen one. As you show the card your left thumb pushes the top one a little way off the pack to the right and you slip the tip of your left little finger beneath at, so as to separate it slightly from the rest of the pack. You next drop the bottom card face up on top of the selected card on top of the pack and, still keeping the little finger beneath the chosen card, you close the other fingers around the two cards so as to square them perfectly together. Now with your right hand you grasp the two cards as though they were one, between the second finger at the far end and the thumb at the near end, and remove them from the pack.

The left thumb now pushes the new top card over to the right so that it overlaps the pack. The left hand edge of the two cards in the right hand (which are held as if they were one) is placed beneath the right hand edge of the top card, and the latter is tipped over to fall face up on the top of the pack as you ask, " Is this the card ? "

The card is then pushed a little to the right by the left thumb and picked up by the right fingers underneath the two cards that they hold, and the next card is turned face up in the same way.

When six or seven cards have been turned over, shown, and taken in the right hand in this way, you appear to lose patience, and say, " Oh well, I give it up. What was your card anyway ? " At the same time you turn all the cards in the right hand face down on top of the pack, which will leave the selected card, face up, six or seven cards down in the pack.

On hearing the name of the selected card you say, " Oh, that card always was a nuisance. We will find it another way."

Cut the pack and then run your thumb rapidly across the edge of it to make a crisp crackling noise. This for effect. Then spread the pack in a long overlapping ribbon of cards so that the chosen one shows, face up, in the middle of the row of face down cards.

SENSITIVE FINGER TIPS

The principle of the corner crimp is used again in our next trick, which is presented as another demonstration of the conjurer's extraordinary sense of touch. The performer appears to succeed in finding, by sense of touch alone, a card which has been simply thought of by a spectator.

Commence by handing the pack to a spectator to shuffle. On receiving it back take the top five cards and, spreading them in a fan, ask the spectator simply to think of one of them. You glance at the cards yourself and remember their order. To do this it is not necessary to remember their complete names and it is far easier not to do so. For instance, I take the five cards from the top of the pack that lies beside me as I write, which happen to be the Queen of Diamonds, King of Spades, seven of Clubs, four of hearts, and five of Clubs, and I simply remember Queen, King, seven, four, and five. It is only necessary to remember suits when two or more cards of the same value appear amongst the five.

When the spectator has thought of a card you close the fan and secretly crimp the corner of the batch of five cards. Then you cut the pack, drop the five crimped cards on the bottom half, and replace the upper half above them. You then take the pack and shuffle it, when you will find that it is very easy to shuffle without separating the five, which will hang together in one batch because of their crimped corners. Finally you cut the cards, so as to bring the five crimped ones to the top of the pack, and you put the pack into the inside breast pocket of your coat, which it is wise to empty for the purpose of this trick.

You now " build up " your effect. That is to say, you enumerate the preceding stages of the trick to impress upon the spectators the remarkable nature of what is being done. A card has been selected by being simply thought of and has been thoroughly shuffled into the pack. Only one person knows the identity of the card. The pack is out of sight in your pocket and only your remarkable sense of touch can aid you to find the card.

Now you ask the spectator to name his card and, as soon as you hear its name you know its position. For example (using the cards we have already mentioned) you repeat to yourself Queen, King, seven, four, five and you know if the selected card is the first, second, third, fourth, or fifth from the top of the pack in your pocket. You put your hand into your pocket, count down to the required number, and slowly draw out the selected card.

THOUGHT DIVINED

We have previously called your attention to the excellent ruse of preparing for one trick while performing another, and we will now give you another example of its efficacy. At the close of the preceding trick the pack was in your inside coat pocket and, as you remove it you leave behind two cards in preparation for the present mystery, which links up well with the last.

You hand the pack to another spectator requesting him to shuffle it and then to hand you any three cards. You hold the cards in front of him in a fan and ask him to think of one of them. Once more you remember the order of the cards.

You now pretend to put the three cards into your inner coat pocket but actually, hidden by your coat, you thrust them into the upper right hand vest pocket and then let your finger tips enter the coat pocket. At this moment you open your coat a little so that the spectators may see the fingers leaving the coat pocket.

In the last trick you found a card that had been thought of, using only your sense of touch. In this one you are going to discover which of the three cards were thought of. You ask the spectator to fix his mind upon his card. You gaze at him earnestly as though you were endeavouring to read his mind and, after a moment, you put your hand into your coat pocket and remove one of the cards you left there at the start. You glance at it (without letting it be seen) nod to yourself as though you were satisfied, and replace it on the pack, saying, " I don't think you are thinking of that one."

You go through the same performance again, as convincingly as you can. First you read the man's mind, then you remove the second card from the coat pocket and return it to the pack, saying " And not that one either."

You continue : " And before I show you that I have succeeded would you mind naming the card you thought of." As soon as you hear its name you know if it is the first, second, or third card in your vest pocket. You keep your coat over the pocket as you quickly find the correct card and draw it out.

PALMING

The technique of card conjuring, as we have mentioned before, has been practically revolutionized during the last fifty years. The nineteenth century conjurer almost invariably controlled a selected card by using the Two Handed Pass, generally bringing it to the top of the pack. He would then palm the card, that is to say he would conceal it in his hand, and he would hand the pack to a spectator to be shuffled. When he received the cards back he would replace the palmed one on the top of the pack and proceed with his trick.

This procedure is excellent but, while it is still used at times by some of the experts, it has gone somewhat out of fashion. The general tendency today is for the conjurer to shuffle the cards himself, thus considerably speeding up the action of his trick.

But there are occasions when it greatly strengthens a trick to allow the spectators to shuffle the pack, and there are other tricks to which palming is essential, so we will give you a method. It would be possible to give you a hundred methods but not very useful to do so. Ever since card tricks and card games were invented the hunt had been on for an indetectible method of palming . . . . and the hunt is still on. We are always appreciative of efforts to extend the technique of conjuring but we feel that the existing methods of palming are quite adequate if the conjurer knows his real business, which is to conduct himself in such a manner that at the moment he is palming his card or his cards the attention of the spectators is diverted to something else. So we shall teach you a comparatively simple but excellent method of palming which you can use for either one or a number of cards. First examine Figure 4, which shows a card in the

FIG 4

palm of the hand. It stretches from the first joints of the fingers almost to the heel of the hand, which is slightly bent in a *natural* manner. The card bends to follow the curve of the hand. Notice now the position of the thumb, which is *relaxed*. A great fault of many amateurs is to stick the thumb

FIG 5

out stiffly, as in Figure 5, when they have palmed a card, and
the unnatural appearance of the hand " telegraphs " the fact
to all the spectators. Of course, when a card is palmed the
back of the hand must always be kept towards the audience,
but that, alone, is not sufficient. The hand must be held and
used in a natural way, so that the presence of the card is not
even suspected.

To palm the top card of the pack you proceed in this
way. Hold the pack in the left hand in the position
for dealing and, with the left thumb, push the top card about
three-eighths of an inch to the right, so that it overlaps the
side of the pack. Bring the right hand over the pack as if to
grasp it by its ends, fingers at the far end and thumb at the
near end. The tips of the first three fingers should rest against
the far end of the pack so that the crease lines which show
where the fingers bend will rest against the edge of the top
card. As the little finger is shorter than the others its tip will
now rest upon the far right hand corner of the top card. We
hope you have a pack of cards in your hands as you read our
description and can ascertain that the facts are as we have
stated them. Press gently down with the right little finger
upon the far right hand corner of the top card and, since it is
overlapping the pack, it will be levered up into the palm of
the hand. It will be necessary to raise the left thumb very
slightly to let the card do this, and the less the thumb moves
the more imperceptible will be your palming. As soon as
the card strikes the inside of the right hand the hand con-
tracts very slightly to secure it, and then grasps the pack and

FIG 6

moves away with it as shown in Figure 6. To the spectators
it should appear that the pack was simply taken from the
left hand into the right.

When it is required to palm a number of cards a little
preliminary action is necessary. Let the right fingers and
thumb rest naturally upon the ends of the pack while the
left thumb counts off the number of cards it is desired to palm
by pushing them off the pack a little way to the right. Square
them up and leave them overlapping the pack about three-
eighths of an inch. Now let the right hand leave the pack,
to make some gesture or perform some action, and then
bring it back to the pack to palm the batch of cards exactly
as if it were only one.

The difficulty in learning to palm is mainly psychological.
The beginner lacks confidence, thinks that the action is too
obvious, holds his hands too tensely, feels self-conscious, and
generally fumbles the job. You must practise the simple
movement until you can do it almost unconsciously, remembering that the only source of confidence is reliance in
your own ability.

We will now give you a few tricks to exercise your skill in
this new acquisition.

HYPNOTISM !

You ask the company if they believe in the possibility of
mass hypnotism and assure them that, at times, the thing is
possible. You will try an experiment ! Very solemnly you
make " hypnotic passes " towards them and you then request
that one of them select a card from the pack and show it to

the others. You have the card replaced in the pack and you bring it secretly to the top, either by using the Pick Up Control or by means of the Corner Crimp and a simple cut. Then you palm the selected card from the top as you take the pack in your right hand, and you tell your audience your story.

"A card has been selected," you say, "while you were all under hypnotic influence." You return the pack to the left hand and spread it in a fan, all the while keeping the selected card palmed, and you continue, "As a matter of fact, it was this card." You remove a card from the fan and show it to the company as in Figure 7, which shows your own view. Observe how you boldly use the hand which palms the card,

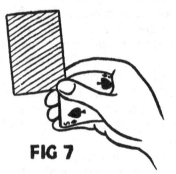

FIG 7

so boldly that none will ever suspect its presence! You continue, "Undoubtedly all of you being under hypnotic influence believe that the card you saw was some other one. What, by the way, was the card you thought was chosen?" On hearing its name you say, "Let me prove to you that you never really saw that card by showing you that I put it into my pocket before we started." Without haste you replace the card you hold on the top of the pack and thrust your hand, with the palmed card into your pocket and withdraw it, holding the selected card!

We commenced the last sentence with the words "without haste." Please read it again because those two words are most important. Beginners are generally in too much hurry when they have a card palmed. It seems to burn the flesh and make them anxious to be rid of it. Remember that, in conjuring, quick movements always attract attention and, perhaps because of the old untruth " the quickness of the hand deceives the eye," quick movements are always suspected. You must carefully practise this action of pretending to take the card from your pocket. You must particularly watch to see that when the hand moves to the pocket its back always remains towards the audience so that they have not the slightest glimpse of the card. Once the hand is safely within the pocket the card is released from the palm and retaken at the finger tips.

THE CARD IN THE POCKET

This is a trick which has enjoyed considerable popularity amongst conjurers and is very puzzling to the spectators. You first hand the pack to one of the company to shuffle and then you ask him to think of a number. You suggest that he should think of a number under twenty in order to save time. You now turn your back upon him and instruct him to quietly count down in the pack and remember the card that lies at the number of his choice, and to replace the cards counted. You tell him to count very quietly so that you will not be able to hear the cards fall and you ask him to tell you when he has finished his task. Then you turn and take the pack from him. You hold it behind you for a moment while you appear to be deep in thought. You then remove a card from near the bottom of the pack and bring it forward, its back to the spectators so that none can see what card it is, and you pretend to put it into your pocket. Actually, as soon as the hand is in the pocket, you palm the card and bring it out again. You immediately take the pack in the hand that is palming the card and, as you place the pack on the table in front of the assisting spectator you add the card to the top of the pack.

Now you build up your effect by pointing out how remarkable it would be if, without any clue and without asking a single question, you had succeeded in finding a card, chosen by merely thinking of a number, and had placed that card in your pocket.

You pick up the pack and ask the assisting spectator to tell you, for the first time, the number he thought of. Let us suppose he says " Fourteen." You deal thirteen cards down on to the table, slowly and deliberately, and place the fourteenth in front of him, saying, " This should be the card you remembered, the fourteenth. What card was it ? " When he has named it you ask him to turn up the card in front of him and he finds, of course, that it is a different one, because you have added one card to the top of the pack. The card he remembered is now on the top of the pack. As he turns up the card on the table and everyone is watching him, you quietly palm the top card of the pack. Then you calmly put your hand into your pocket and withdraw it holding the palmed card at the finger-tips : and another miracle has been accomplished.

THINK OF A NUMBER

We are reminded of another excellent trick in which a spectator counts down to his chosen number, as in the last, but the general effect is quite different.

First secretly crimp the bottom card of the pack, as we have already taught you, and then shuffle it to the top. Hand the pack to a spectator and ask him to think of a number. Again suggest a number under twenty, to save time. When he has made his mental choice turn your back and tell him to deal that number of cards noiselessly on to the table. When he tells you he has done that, tell him to show the card that remains on top of the pack to the rest of the company, to replace it, to replace the cards he has dealt, to cut the pack, and to complete the cut.

Turn and take the pack from him, remarking that the card having been selected and replaced under test conditions, all your powers will be required to find it. Actually, as you will have discovered if you have performed the actions yourself, the selected card lies beneath the one with the crimped corner.

Look at the end of the pack. The crimped card will show quite plainly to one who knows what he is looking for. Cut the pack so that the crimped card becomes the bottom one, and the selected card will be on top. False shuffle so as to leave the card there and then ask for its name.

Slide the top card, the chosen one, to the right so that it overlaps the pack about an inch. Immediately grasp the pack with the right hand, by its ends, and slap it down upon the table. The pressure of the air against the overlapping card will cause it to turn over and appear, face up, upon the top of the pack.

This last effect is a very old way of revealing a selected card and is generally called " The Revolution." A little experiment will be necessary before the effect becomes quite certain. The pack should be tossed on to the table from a distance of about eighteen inches, and not too violently. But it is not sufficient to " let fall the pack " as a famous author has said when describing the trick.

EDUCATED FINGERS

Still using the principles we have taught you already, we give you now a beautiful trick which combines some classic card technique with modern simplified methods. The effect, as the audience see it, is that two cards are chosen and replaced in the pack, which is then shuffled by a spectator. The pack is then put into the performer's pocket and the two cards are found by his educated fingers.

You begin by letting two people each draw a card from the pack, and while they are showing their cards to the rest of the company you crimp the corner of the bottom card and cut the pack to bring the bottom card to the centre. Then you cut the pack at the crimped corner and have the first selected card replaced, dropping the cut back on top of it. You repeat this with the second card and then cut at the crimp once more to bring both cards to the top of the pack. Next you palm the two cards from the pack and hand it to a spectator to shuffle thoroughly.

With your right hand, which holds the two palmed cards, pull out the lining of your trousers pocket and show it empty. Replace the pocket and leave the two cards within it. Leave the cards standing on their ends. Take the pack from the shuffler and put it into the pocket also. Leave the pack on its *side*. Thus the two cards already in the pocket will not become mixed with the pack.

Ask the name of the first selected card. Put your hand into your pocket and pretend to feel for the card in the pack. After a moment or two bring out the card you require. Remember that if you had the cards replaced in the order in which they were taken the first selected card will be the second card in your pocket.

Produce the other card in the same way.

There we have what Professor Hoffmann called " the bare bones " of the trick—the first essentials, the foundations upon which one has to build. We will now examine our procedure in more detail.

When cutting at the crimp for the selected cards to be returned try to make your cut as late as possible. That is to say do not cut the pack long before the spectator is ready to return his card. He may become suspicious and try to return it to another part of the pack. The pack should rest naturally in the left hand. You ask the selector of the card if he will replace it and you extend the left hand towards him. As he holds out his card you cut the pack, using only the second finger and thumb of the right hand. The thumb finds the crimp almost automatically and the cut is made without hesitation at the correct spot. The selector replaces his card upon the lower portion and you *drop* the upper portion on top of it, letting it fall four or five inches, to land with an audible " smack ". This emphasises the apparent fairness of the procedure and makes the subsequent discovery of the card all the more remarkable.

The next point to watch is the palming of the two cards after they have been brought to the top of the pack. It is best done as you move towards the person you ask to shuffle the pack. It is a simple matter to push the two cards a little to the right in readiness for the palm. Speak directly to a member of the audience seated on your left and ask him if he will shuffle the pack. As you move towards him palm the cards in your right hand and take the pack in the same hand, holding it by its ends, and give him the pack. Your own inclination would be to give him the pack with the other hand, the empty one, but this would be quite wrong. Give him the pack with the right hand and hold the left so that he can see it is empty and he will not dream that you are withholding any cards.

Your technical troubles are now nearly over. But you must be careful how you hold your hand as you pull out and replace the lining of your trouser pocket. Try this over, half a dozen times, in front of your wardrobe mirror.

When you receive the pack from the shuffler hold it at the tips of the fingers and let all the audience see that you place it deliberately and fairly into the pocket. But do not make any remarks about this. It is always a mistake to say " Observe that my hands are empty . . . . notice that I do not do anything tricky " . . . and so on. Such remarks only remind the audience of the possibility of trickery and spoil the enjoyment of good conjuring. And we hope your conjuring will be good.

Finally, when you are producing the cards from the pocket try to act as if you were really finding them in the shuffled pack . . . . finding two particular cards amongst fifty-two. And we think that you will find that your acting will be more convincing if you appear to be just a little bit astonished at your own success.

FALSE SHUFFLING IV

When the top stock is rather large, that is to say when you desire to keep in place on the top of the pack a fairly large number of cards, the Top Stock Pick Up Shuffle is not the best method to use, in fact seven or eight cards is the most that should be retained by that means.

To keep a *large* stock undisturbed, take the pack in the left hand in the usual shuffling position and undercut beneath

the number of cards you wish to retain. Bring the right hand
down to shuffle off and, with the left thumb, draw off the first
card of the right hand packet so that it overlaps the left hand
packet (the top stock) about three-eighths of an inch at the
end nearer yourself. Then shuffle off the remaining cards.
The pack will now be in the left hand with the top stock at the
bottom separated from the rest of the pack by one card which
protrudes at the near end, as depicted in Figure 8. Cut the

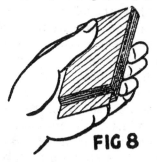

FIG 8

pack by picking up with the right hand the protruding card
and all those above it. Complete the cut and your top stock
will once more be in place.

A card left protruding from the pack in this manner is
called, in the jargon of the craft, a " jogged " card. It is " in-
jogged " when it protrudes from the near end of the pack and
" out-jogged " when it protrudes from the far end. A false
shuffle using this principle is a " jog shuffle " and the simple
one we have just taught you is the Top Stock Jog Shuffle.
Some very marvellous things may be done by shuffles based
on this principle . . . . but that is another story.

SPELL IT OUT

We shall now return for a while to the idea of knowing the
card which is on the bottom of the pack and using it for a key
card. We shall acquaint you with some variations of that idea
in this and the succeeding sections.

To discover a selected card by spelling its name has been,
for long, a favourite effect with conjurers. As you spell the

name of the card, you deal one card for each letter, and the selected card is reached with the last letter of its name.

One of the simplest methods for achieving this effect is very similar to the one which we have already described for finding a card at a chosen number. (See " The Card and the Number.") You bring the chosen card to the top of the pack, which you hand to the chooser. You tell him to spell out the name of his card and to deal one card for each letter. He is to turn up the last card. Of course, the card he turns up is not the chosen one, and you blame him for not doing the trick properly. You replace the cards and show him how he should have done it. You deal one card for each letter of the name and turn up the selected card as you pronounce the last letter. The first attempt has put the card into the correct position.

The weakness of this method is that it can only be used once before the same people. After that they would be rather suspicious regarding the preliminary failure. We will give you another method.

If you examine the question of the number of letters required to spell the different cards of the pack you will find that all, except the Joker, may be spelt with eight, nine, ten, eleven, twelve, or thirteen letters when spelt in full as, for example, " Ace of Spades ", and that even the Joker can be spelt with thirteen if you call him " The Jolly Joker." Here is the table :

Ace, two, six, and ten of Clubs . . . . . eight letters

Ace, two, six, and ten of Hearts and Spades,
four, five, nine, Jack, and King of Clubs . . . . . nine letters.

Three, seven, eight, and Queen of Clubs,
four, five, nine, Jack and King of Hearts and Spades . . . . .
ten letters.

Ace, two, six, and ten of Diamonds,
three, seven, eight, and Queen of Hearts and Spades . . . . .
eleven letters.

Four, five, nine, Jack and King of Diamonds . . . . .twelve
letters.

Three, seven, eight, and Queen of Diamonds . . . . . thirteen
letters.

Or perhaps you will find this a more convenient form :—

Clubs . . . . five letters
Hearts and Spades . . . . six letters
Diamonds . . . . eight letters
Ace, two, six, and ten . . . . .three letters
Four, five, nine, Jack, and King . . . . . four letters
Three, seven, eight, and Queen . . . . . .five letters.

Armed with this information you are able to perform the spelling trick in a different way.

Begin by spreading the cards between your hands and asking a spectator to select one. As you spread the cards, by pushing them to the right with your left thumb, you count them and separate the first twelve from the others. When the selector has made his choice you close the pack and hold a break under the twelfth card with the tip of your left little finger. After the selector has shown his card to the company you cut the pack at the break and ask him to return his card. You drop the cut on top of his card, square up the pack very deliberately, and make your Top Stock Jog Shuffle. The chosen card will then be the thirteenth from the top of the pack. To the minds of the spectators it is hopelessly lost in the pack.

You tell your audience that you have a most intelligent and well-educated pack. The cards even know how to spell their own names. You enquire the name of the selected card. If it is either the three, seven, eight, or Queen of Diamonds (or even the Joker) you simply run your fingers across the edge of the pack to make a sharp crackling noise, purely for " effect ", and hand the cards to the selector, telling him to deal one card for each letter of the name of the one he selected.

Should the card be any of the others you must calculate how many cards you must remove from the top of the pack to produce your effect. You do this by showing the selector how you wish him to count the cards by dealing them on to the table one by one so that everyone may follow. If the card is spelt with eight letters (ace, two, six, and ten of Clubs) you deal five cards in explanation. You pick up these cards and put them back *on the bottom of the pack*. Then you hand the pack to the selector for him to spell his card. For a nine letter card you would deal four, for a ten letter card three, and so on.

There are some people to whom all calculations are abhorrent and for whom the task of deducting four from thirteen is too difficult. There are others who find it impossible to remember the values of the cards and to work out the numbers of their letters, or at least, to do so quickly. We must confess that we have never liked work of this sort, either of memory or of calculation, when in the presence of an audience. When the Author is giving a conjuring show he wishes to be free to give the whole of his mind to the things he says and the way in which he says them, and he does not wish to be worried with either calculation or recollection. If you are like him you may prefer the following method, which makes use once more of the principle of the key card.

Invite a spectator to choose a card and, while he is showing it to the company, glance at the bottom card of the pack, remember it, and cut the cards so as to bring this key card to the centre of the pack, keeping a break below it with the tip of the little finger. Cut the pack at the break, let the card be replaced, drop the cut back on top, and square up the pack. The selected card is now beneath your key card.

Make a quick movement of the hands and run your thumb across the edge of the pack so as to make a rustling noise and arouse the suspicions of the audience. Stop, and say : " I beg your pardon. I hope you do not think I have done anything to your card. Let me show you it is still in the pack." Turn the pack face upwards and pass the cards from your left hand to your right hand one by one, showing their faces. Watch for your key card, the original bottom one. The one beneath it, the one to the right in the face up pack, is the selected card. Beginning with the key card, spell the name of the selected card to yourself as you pass the cards one by one from left to right. Omit the final " S " of the name of the suit, and when you come to the penultimate letter, look at the spectator and say : " Have you seen your card ? " and, as he replies to you, cut the pack to bring the last card you reached to the top. Now make the Top Stop Jog Shuffle and hand the pack to the selector for him to spell his card.

There is an extension of this idea which, we think, considerably improves it. You proceed exactly as above but when you run through the pack to show the cards you first spell to yourself, as you count, the name of the selected card, then you note the name of the card you reach when you arrive at the final " S ", and then you spell that card also, omitting the " S ". Let us suppose this final card is the king of Hearts. You cut the pack and you tell the spectator who chose the card that you are going to give him the power to find his card by spelling its name. First you will show him how to do it. " For instance," you say, " if I want to find the King of Hearts I concentrate my mind upon that card and flip the pack, so. Then I deal one card for each letter of its name, so . . . .

K - I - N - G - O - F - H - E - A - R - T - S

and the King turns up." You deal the King face up as you pronounce the letter S.

Now you hand the pack to the spectator and make him concentrate his mind upon his card and spell and find it for himself.

THE MARKED CARD

This principle of the Key card has many variations, such as that of the Marked Card, to which we now introduce you You will often notice, when you are doing card tricks with a pack that has been used for games, a card with a definite mark upon its back, a cracked corner, or a spot of some sort. If you do not notice such a card you can always manufacture one by pressing your thumbnail into the corner of a card.

With your marked card, found by chance or made to order, on the bottom of the pack, you proceed exactly as we have already taught you. You have a card selected, you cut to take your key card to the centre of the pack, and you have the selected card replaced beneath the key. You can now shuffle the pack if you take care not to shuffle the centre portion, so that the selected card will remain beneath the key card.

An excellent way of proceeding then is to put the shuffled pack on the table and ask the selector to cut it into six or seven small packets. When he has done this ask him if he can tell in which of the packets his card lies. Undoubtedly he will say that he has no idea. Ask him to choose one of the packets. Spread the packet he chooses into an overlapping row and run the tips of your fingers along it, while you half close your eyes and behave as if this slight contact of the finger tips were conveying some information to you. Meanwhile you are looking for the marked card and as soon as you have ascertained that it is not within the packet you tell the selector that his card is not there, and ask him to choose another packet. Proceed in this way until you find the packet with the marked card and then announce the presence of the selected one.

Keeping track of the selected card, which you know is the one beneath the marked one, you spread the cards haphazardly over the table, using both hands. You take the spectator by the wrist and ask him to concentrate his mind upon the identity of his card. You steer his hand in a circular movement over the cards and then gradually decrease the size of the circle until it diminishes to a point directly above the selected card. You suddenly put the spectator's hand upon his card and let him turn it up.

You can imagine how strong the effect is, and often the spectator will examine the card, vainly seeking a clue to the mystery.

FROM THE FAN

We now come to another variation of the principle of the key card, one which is quite different from any that have gone before.

You hand the pack to a member of the audience to be shuffled, and, when you receive it back, you take the top ten or twelve cards and put the rest of the pack on the table. As you do so you glance at and remember the bottom card of your packet of ten or twelve.

Now you mix your packet of cards together in a casual way, using both hands, and you so contrive that at the end of the mixing your noted card will be the top card of the packet. You should not have any real difficulty in doing this. Now you spread the packet of cards into a very wide fan, so that all the cards are well separated from each other, and holding the fan in one hand, you invite a spectator to lift up one card by its corner, to peep at its index, and to remember its name. As the spectator does this you count and remember the number of cards between your key card, on top of the fan, and the card which the spectator peeps at.

You then close the fan of cards and, cutting the pack, bury the packet of ten or twelve within. Finally you cut the pack several times, each time completing the cut.

The position now is that the key card is lost somewhere in the pack and that the selected card follows it, separated by a certain number of cards which you know. You have only to find the key card to be able to find the selected one also.

It would be interesting to leave you to devise your own continuation to the trick but as we should be unable to enjoy the results, or even know if you arrived at any, we had better, perhaps, provide you with a conclusion.

If when you replaced the packet within the pack, you put it somewhere near the centre, and if, when you cut the pack, you did so an even number of times, the selected card and the key will be still somewhere towards the centre of the pack. Verify that please, while we wait a moment . . . . . Then if you cut the pack into three portions you may be fairly sure that the selected card and the key card will be in that portion which was the centre of the pack ? Good !

Cut the pack into three portions then and ask the selector if he has any notion as to which of the heaps contains his card. When he replies in the negative suggest that the centre heap be tried. Say : " I will just show you the cards in this heap. After I have shown you all the cards, but not before, tell me if your card is in this heap." Now you deal the cards into a face up pile and you count them as you deal. Let us suppose that there were six cards between the key and the selected card. As you deal, and count, your key card turns up, say, at the sixth card, you count on six more, and the next, the thirteenth, is the selected card. You remember its name, and you complete the dealing.

You ask the spectator if his card is in the heap, and when he replies in the affirmative, you turn the cards face downwards and hand them to him. You turn your back and hold your hands behind you and you ask the spectator to deal the cards on to your hands, one by one. As you feel the cards being dealt on to your hands you count them and, after the twelfth has arrived and before the thirteenth, you suddenly cry : "Stop ! You are holding your card ! Am I right ? "

You pause for a moment to permit the spectators to applaud if they wish to, as they should, and then you continue : " Now let me see if I can discover the name of your card. Put the card into your pocket so that I cannot see it, will you ? " When he has done that turn to face him and say : " I want you to think of the identity of that card and I will try to divine it." (Let us suppose for the sake of our description that the card is the three of Spades.) " First, let us see, is the card red or black ? It is black I think. Yes, I see from your eyes that it is black. A Club or a Spade, that is the question ? I will take a chance and say it is a Spade. It is. Now it might be a court card or a pip card. King, Queen, Jack . . . . no, I see it is a pip card. The ace ? No. The two ? No. The Three ? Yes ! It's the three. Am I right ? Thank you ! "

In some such fashion and with some such words, which will be much more effective than simply blurting out its name, you divine the card. If you act your part well, a good proportion of your spectators will half believe that you can read the man's mind, and will be willing and *pleased to believe it*. It is this that we meant when we said in our Preface that the art of the conjurer lies in dressing up his tricks. And when those tricks are well dressed up the spectators will find pleasure in believing in the reality of magic even though the belief only lasts while the performance continues.

THE SPECTATOR DOES IT

The variations of this theme of the discovery of the chosen card are almost as many as the variations which there are in the use of this principle of the key card. In the trick which we shall now give you the selector of the card appears to find it for himself.

First you have a card selected and, while it is being shown to the company, you turn your back so that you cannot see what card it is. While your back is turned you quietly turn the bottom card of the pack face upwards, cut to bring it to the centre, and hold a break beneath it with the tip of your little finger. You now turn back to the audience and have the card replaced, cutting at the break so that it is replaced beneath the reversed card, and dropping the cut back in the manner which should now be quite familiar to you. Your trick will be improved if you then give the cards a shuffle, taking care not to disturb the centre of the pack where the two cards lie.

In this, and in all tricks in which cards are secretly reversed in the pack, it is best to use cards the backs of which have plain white margins rather than the popular pictorial cards, now so much in vogue, upon which the colouring extends to the edge of the card. With these cards one must keep the pack very carefully squared up if the reversed one is not to be seen at the wrong moment, while with the white margin cards there is nothing to be feared even should the pack be slightly spread out.

But to return to our trick. You continue by asking the chooser to step forward and face the audience with you, and you tell him that you wish him to try a simple experiment with you, or rather, a not so simple experiment. You say to him : " I want you to hold the pack behind your back like this, and to do exactly as I tell you." In illustration you put the cards behind you, and you quickly turn the second card from the top face upwards. Then you hand the pack to the chooser and give him your instructions. " Hold the pack behind your back please. Keep it there all the while so that none can see exactly how this is done. Now take the top card and.... no ! better not use that one .... put that on the bottom of the pack and take the next one. Now turn that card face up and thrust it into the pack, *anywhere you like.* Have you done that ? Good. Square up the pack please and then give it to me."

Now you turn to the audience and explain what has been done so that they may appreciate the truly marvellous nature of the effect. First a card was chosen at random and put back in the pack, which has been shuffled. The selector of the card has thrust a second card, face upwards, into the pack. And now comes the miracle. In some such words you make sure that the spectators really appreciate the worth of your trick. You must always do this. The conjurer who does not blow his own trumpet will find nobody else to do it for him.

You now take the pack and spread it in a fan until the reversed card can be seen. You are careful to do this slowly and deliberately so that all can see that you do not manipulate the cards in any way. You remove the reversed card and the card beneath it together, and you ask the name of the selected card. You slowly turn over the two cards you hold to show that the chooser has found his own card.

You can see, of course, what really happened. It is your original reversed bottom card which is next to the selected one. The card the chooser thrusts into the pack is the second one from the top which you had turned face upwards and which he turns face downwards, thus losing it in the pack.

TURN OVER

Here is another trick which bears some similarity to the last in that a card is found by another which is reversed.

The procedure is similar also. You have a card selected and you turn away while it is being shown to the company. While you turn your back you cut the pack to bring either a seven, an eight, a nine, or a ten to the bottom. You then turn this card over and count off the same number of cards as its value, reversing the order of these cards as you do so and finally replacing them on the bottom of the pack. That is to say, supposing that you bring an eight to the bottom of the pack, you first turn the eight face upwards, then you count off eight cards, taking the second on top of the first, the third on top of the second, and so on, and replace the eight cards on the bottom of the pack. The result is to leave the reversed eight, eight cards from the bottom of the pack.

Now you turn to the audience again and cut the pack, holding the break beneath the cut in the usual fashion. You have the selected card replaced beneath the cut and you have nothing more to do than to " work up " the effect.

You explain that you are going to ask one of the cards to turn over in the pack and that that card will enable you to find the selected one. You run your thumb across the edge of the cards and spread the pack in a fan until the reversed one appears. You cut the pack to make the reversed card the top one and call attention to the number of its pips, eight. You count down eight cards and ask the name of the selected one ; then you turn it over to show that another marvel has been produced.

THE FORECAST

Sometimes, instead of finding a selected card the conjurer forecasts the card that will be chosen and this, astonishingly enough, may also be done by the aid of our old friend, the bottom card of the pack.

You tell your audience that, after very many years of patient research, you have discovered a method of foretelling with comparative certainty the events that will occur in the immediate future. Unfortunately the events must occur within the very immediate future and your present time limit is within five minutes of your forecast. This limitation of time is extremely annoying and has kept you, up to now, from giving up work and making a real clean up on the football pools. However, it is rather interesting and you will give a demonstration of your ability with the pack of cards.

You take the pack and glance at the bottom card. You remember its name and you shuffle it to the top. Now, keeping the pack in your left hand, you take an envelope and a slip of paper and, using the pack to support the paper, you write on the latter, " The lady will cut the cards at the .... of.... " writing, of course, the name of the card you noted, now on the top of the pack. Of course, if you are performing amongst friends you would write the name of the lady you intend to ask to assist in this trick. The slip of paper you now seal in the envelope and, while you are doing this, you take the opportunity to push the top card a little over the side of the pack. Then, when you have pressed the flap of the envelope well down to seal it, which gives you an excuse to place the envelope on top of the pack again, you are able, very simply, to carry the card away beneath the envelope as you take the latter in your right hand. This card beneath the envelope is, of course, the one whose name is written upon the slip of paper within.

Now, with the pack resting upon the palm of the outstretched left hand, you advance to the lady and ask her to cut the cards wherever she wishes. Impress upon her that she has perfect freedom to cut high or low, as she prefers. When she has cut the cards you say, " We will mark the cut with the envelope for a moment," and you put the envelope, with the card beneath it, on the bottom half of the pack, and ask the lady to replace the top half above the envelope. Then you hand the lady the pack, with the envelope sandwiched within it, asking her to hold them for a moment.

Now you recapitulate. A moment or two ago you wrote a forecast which you sealed in the envelope. The lady has now cut the pack at a point she freely chose, and nobody knows what card lies at that point. Could anyone have known beforehand ?

You ask the lady to lift up the envelope and to tell the company what card it is at which she has cut. When she has done that you ask her to open the envelope and read aloud your forecast ......

A CARD PUZZLE
We will conclude Part I of our handbook with an excellent puzzle with cards which is well worth showing if you will take

the trouble to learn it properly. It is done with the twelve
court cards and aces and the object is to lay them out in four
rows of four cards so that in none of the rows, hori-
zontal or vertical, shall there be two cards of either the
same value or the same suit. A possible arrangement is
shown below :

Queen of Diamonds	Ace of Clubs	Jack of Hearts	King of Spades
Ace of Hearts	Queen of Spades	King of Diamonds	Jack of Clubs
Jack of Spades	King of Hearts	Queen of Clubs	Ace of Diamonds
King of Clubs	Jack of Diamonds	Ace of Spades	Queen of Hearts

All the explanations of this puzzle which we have seen tell
you to begin by setting up the two diagonals with four cards
of the same value, but this spoils the whole thing by making
it appear too easy. Actually, even when the diagonals are set
up, the thing is not so simple as it appears to be.

We are going to show you how to lay out the cards from
left to right in four rows, explaining all the points it is necessary
to remember in order to do so. We think the best way to do
this will be for us to actually lay out the cards as we would if
we were showing the puzzle to some friends. So we first take
the court cards and aces from the pack and shuffle them
thoroughly. Now we turn the cards face upwards and take
the first one, which we put down on the table in what will be
the top left hand corner of our square of cards. The card
happens to be the Jack of Diamonds. The next card is the
King of Clubs which we put down beside the Jack. The third
card is the Jack of Clubs, which we pass by, since we have
already both a Jack and a Club in the row and, in any case,
the cards must be alternately red and black ones. The next
card is the Ace of Hearts, which we put beside the King. Now

a glance at these cards shows that to complete the row we require a Queen, and a second glance shows that it must be the Queen of Spades, so we find that card to make the first line . . . .

| Jack of | King of | Ace of | Queen of |
| Diamonds | Clubs | Hearts | Spades |

Now the second line must always commence with a card of the same value as the second card of the first line, but of the opposite colour. In the present case it must be a red king and, since the first vertical has already been started with the Jack of Diamonds we must use the King of Hearts. Now the two diagonals must consist of cards of the same value and the centre cards must be of the opposite colour to the corner ones. Our next card must therefore be a black jack, and as the King of Clubs heads the second vertical line we must put down the Jack of Spades. Our rule about the diagonal tells us that the next card must be a red queen and as the Queen of Hearts will not do we can only put down the Queen of Diamonds. An ace is needed to complete the line and must obviously be the Ace of Clubs. Our second line is completed then, and we have . . . .

Jack of	King of	Ace of	Queen of
Diamonds	Clubs	Hearts	Spades
King of	Jack of	Queen of	Ace of
Hearts	Spades	Diamonds	Clubs

The third line must always commence with a card of the same value as the third card of the first line. It must therefore be an ace and, as we have already two red cards in the first vertical line, we put down our remaining black ace, the Ace of Spades. Our next two cards will be determined by the rule of the diagonal and can only be the Queen of Hearts and the Jack of Clubs. The King of Diamonds must complete the line, giving us . . . .

Jack of	King of	Ace of	Queen of
Diamonds	Clubs	Hearts	Spades
King of	Jack of	Queen of	Ace of
Hearts	Spades	Diamonds	Clubs
Ace of	Queen of	Jack of	King of
Spades	Hearts	Clubs	Diamonds

It requires very little thought to see how one must arrange
the last four cards to complete the magic square so . . . .

Jack of Diamonds	King of Clubs	Ace of Hearts	Queen of Spades
King of Hearts	Jack of Spades	Queen of Diamonds	Ace of Clubs
Ace of Spades	Queen of Hearts	Jack of Clubs	King of Diamonds
Queen of Clubs	Ace of Diamonds	King of Spades	Jack of Hearts

With a little practice you will become so expert at laying out
the puzzle that you will be able to deal the cards almost without
hesitation, while your friends will find it very difficult to do
even though they start with the two diagonal lines.

PART II

WE will commence the second half of our Handbook with a simple piece of sleight-of-hand, of very great utility, which we shall ask you to learn before you go any further. You should find no difficulty in doing so. In this Handbook we do not ask you to learn anything that requires much dexterity. This piece of sleight-of-hand is called

THE GLIDE

and its object is to enable you apparently to deal the bottom card of the pack while in reality you slide that back a little and deal, in its place, the second card from the bottom.

It is done in this way. You hold the pack by its sides in the left hand, between the forefinger and the thumb, with the back of the top card facing the palm of the hand. You let the tips of the second and third fingers rest against the face of the bottom card, as in Figure 9. You turn the hand so that the

FIG 9

pack faces the ground and draw back the bottom card about half an inch, as shown in Figure 10, by a simple movement of the second and third fingers.

The right hand second and third finger tips now draw out the second card from the bottom, apparently the bottom one, and drop it on to the table. Then, by reversing the movement

53

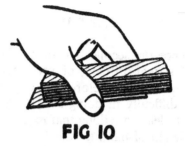

FIG 10

of the fingers the drawn back card may be slid back to its former place.

The Glide may be used to change one card into another as, for example, to change an indifferent card into a selected one. You have a card selected and replaced in the pack and you bring it to the top by means of the corner crimp, for example. You now shuffle the pack by drawing off the top and bottom cards together and shuffling the rest of the pack on top of them, when the selected card will be the second from the bottom. Please try this shuffle before we go on. You will find that it is a combination of the shuffle to take the top card to the bottom and False Shuffle I which leaves the bottom card in place.

Now, holding the pack in position for the Glide, you show the bottom card to the spectators saying, " I suppose the shuffle has not, by any chance, left the selected card on the bottom of the pack ? " As the chooser replies you lower your hand, making the glide, and apparently draw out the card you have just shown and drop it on to the floor. But really it is the second card from the bottom, the selected one which you drop upon the floor. You ask the selector to put his foot upon it.

Now you ask for the name of the selected card and command it to change places with the card on the floor. You cut the pack to bury the card you have shown in the centre and you run your thumb sharply across the edge of the pack before asking the selector to turn up the card beneath his foot.

In the pages that follow we shall give you some further uses for this simple sleight.

THE INSEPARABLE ACES I

To avoid repeatedly having to ask the audience to select cards from the pack the practice has developed of performing tricks with the kings or the aces, which the conjurer removes from the pack himself. Of late years the aces have been most favoured since they are the most conspicuous cards in the pack. In the present trick you use the two red aces.

You run through the pack and pick out the two aces, which you throw down upon the table, and you secretly glance at the top card of the pack and remember its name. You then put the pack down beside the aces and ask one of the spectators, when you have turned your back, to first cut off a small packet of cards and put it upon the table to one side, then to take either of the aces and to place it on top of this small packet, next to cut off a further portion of the pack and to drop it on top of the ace, then to place the other ace upon the last portion, and finally to drop the rest of the pack on top and to square up the cards. You then ask the spectator to cut the pack twice, each time completing the cut.

You now turn round and, taking the pack, point out exactly what has been done. The two aces have been lost in the pack and separated from each other by an unknown number of cards. You hold the pack in the position for the glide and commence to deal the cards from the bottom, dealing them face up upon the table, as you remark that you will demonstrate that the aces are inseparable and, in spite of all, will be found together in the pack.

As you deal the cards from the bottom you watch for the original top card, which you have remembered, and as soon as it appears you know that the next card will be one of the aces. Instead of dealing this ace you make the glide, sliding the card back about half an inch. You must do this without the slightest hesitation or pause and you then continue to deal the cards until the second ace appears, when you at once deal the first ace upon it to show that the aces have come together again.

It will be interesting to ask if you now realize why we told you at the beginning that you use the two red aces in this trick. The point is that in the dénouement the aces are dealt in the reverse order to which they were placed in the pack and if you were to use the black aces this fact might possibly be noticed by a wide awake spectator because of the conspicuous nature of " old mossy face " the Ace of Spades.

THE INSEPARABLE ACES II

The effect is the same as in the last trick, the separated aces come together again, but this time all the four aces are used and all the action of the trick is done by the performer without any assistance from the audience. This is a great advantage in a card trick, and a welcome change from the majority, in which the active participation of the audience is generally required.

To lend a little verisimilitude to the story you will tell of the inability to keep the aces separate it is as well to commence the trick with them all together in the pack. As we pointed out in Part I the best way to manage this would be to get the four aces together in the course of a preceding trick, but another way is to do so as you look through the pack for the Joker. You fan the cards between your hands and hold a break when you come to the first ace. You fan the cards further until you come to the second ace. You draw this out of its position and slide it back beside the first one. You do the same with the third and fourth aces. You ignore the Joker if you come to it before you have found all the aces, as you probably will, and you return to it afterwards. Without comment you discard the Joker. It is probably better to leave the audience wondering why you did this than to give them an explanation that is not entirely convincing.

Now you tell your story : that in a well-trained and properly kept pack of cards the aces are always inseparable. Drag them apart and, as soon as they can, they will fly together again. You fan the pack, the faces of the cards towards the audience, until you come to the aces, all together as you have stated, and you draw them out and drop them upon the table.

Now, holding the pack in your left hand, spread into a wide fan, you push the aces half way into the fan in different parts of it, as shown in Figure 11. Apparently you do this

FIG II

haphazardly but really you take care to remember the name of the card to the right of each of the first three aces. The indices of all the cards being plainly visible when you fan the pack like this you will have no great difficulty but, to facilitate remembering the cards, it is as well to pick out three of the same suit. So, for example, you look along your fan and you see the seven of Hearts, behind which you put your first ace. You go farther along the fan until you come to another Heart, say the four, and you put the second ace behind that. You carry on until you come to, say, the King of Hearts, behind which you put the third ace, and all you need remember now is " seven, four and King of Hearts."

Next you close the fan, leaving the aces still half protruding from the pack so that the spectators can see quite plainly that they are separated from one another. Then holding the pack by its sides, you tap the ends of the aces and drive them slowly into the pack, which you then cut twice, each time completing the cut. You take care, also, to cut at about the centre of the pack each time, so that the two cuts practically neutralize each other and leave the cards as they were, although the spectators, with the trust which the public has in the efficacy of cutting, will not realize this fact.

You remark that although the aces have been well separated it will only take them a few moments to come together again and, holding the pack in the position for the glide, you begin to deal the cards, faces up, from the bottom of the pack. As you deal you watch for the first of your three memorized cards, in our example the seven of Hearts, and, as soon as it appears, you glide back the next card, which you know will be the first ace, and you go on dealing without a pause until you come to the second card which you have remembered.

When you were practising the Glide you probably discovered that an easier way to do the same thing was to push the bottom card back half an inch with the fingers of the right hand instead of pulling it back with the second and third fingers of the left hand. We hope you realized that this method, besides being less elegant, was less good and less undetectable as, always when it is used, there will be a slight hesitation before the card is dealt as the fingers push back the bottom card before drawing out the second one. However, it will be necessary to use that method now and to push back the second ace flush with the first with the right hand fingers, since the position of the first card prevents the use of the Glide. To cover the momentary hesitation before dealing, you deliberately pause, and say to the audience : " Surely we should have reached an ace by now ? "

Then you continue to deal the cards until you reach the third card which you have remembered, the King of Hearts in our example, when you pause once again and say : " Still no aces," as the right fingers push the third ace flush with the first two so that you may continue to deal indifferent cards.

You go on dealing until you actually come to the fourth ace when you say : " At last we have come to the ace, and the other three are with it " . . . . and you deal the three drawn back aces on to the first.

THE FOUR ACES I

Almost everybody has seen and nearly everybody knows the ancient trick with four kings which are shown, spread in a fan, with the three jacks concealed behind them. The fan is closed and the seven cards, apparently four, are dropped on the top of the pack. Now the first "king", really a jack, is taken from the top and slid into the pack a little way down. A second "king", another jack, is pushed into the pack half way down. A third is replaced in the pack three-quarters way down, and the last king, which may be shown, of course, is placed on the bottom of the pack. The pack is then cut and the four kings are discovered all together in the centre. While these childish manœvures are being carried out an infantile story of four burglars is told.

The trick in that form is so well-known that it is not worth doing, although it still appears from time to time in books on conjuring written by the ill-informed for the wholly ignorant. But the trick is the fore-runner of the modern Four Ace Trick, which is so popular that we have been unable to discover a conjurer who has never performed some version of it, and we have been informed that there are over a thousand different versions. In the method we shall describe for you we shall take advantage of the old trick being so well known to have a little fun with the audience.

This trick may well follow the last, in which case you will have the aces separate from the pack, but if it does not you will commence by running through the pack and picking out the four aces. And then you have your joke. You murmur an excuse and turn your back to the audience ! First you take the three top cards of the pack and slip them into your bottom left hand vest pocket, where they remain hidden by your coat. Then you arrange the four aces into a very trim fan which you hold in your right hand in a suspicious way, as if you were hiding something behind it. The pack you keep in your left hand.

Now you turn back to the audience and announce the famous mystery of the four aces.

If you are performing the trick before a small company of people in an ordinary room we suggest that you kneel down and do it all upon the carpet.

You put the pack down on the carpet and then, using both hands, you close the fan of cards rather clumsily and put them on the top of the pack, saying : " The four aces I place on the top of the pack, so." Then you pick up the pack and deal the aces one by one in a row upon the carpet saying : " Now I deal the aces in a row upon the floor." You pause for a moment and add : " Now everyone knows that the aces are in a row on the carpet." Again you pause. The peculiar action and the unnecessary statements will have made everyone dissatisfied that the aces are on the carpet as you say they are. Some expressions of doubt will surely be made. You raise your eyebrows and open your eyes in surprise .... and then you slowly turn over the four cards to show that they really are the aces.

Now you say : " Let's start again." You pick up the aces and place them on top of the pack. You say : " First I deal the aces in a row upon the carpet." You bring your right hand over the pack and grasp it by the ends while you run your thumb across the edge to make a suspicious rustling noise. Then you deal the four aces on to the carpet rather quickly and say : " Well, everyone knows that the aces are there this time."

Again the audience will dissent and after a pause, with an expression of mock amazement, you turn over the four cards to show the aces once more. As you do this you push the top three cards a little to the right of the pack with your left thumb and slip the tip of your little finger beneath them to hold a " break ". You say : " This is very strange. Let us start again."

You gather up the four aces and you drop them on the top of the pack. Then you pause as though a thought had just struck you and say : " I see what it is. You don't think I put the aces on top of the pack." Aided by the break held by the little finger you take the top seven cards in the right hand and put the pack down upon the carpet. Now you take the seven cards in your left hand, holding them at the finger tips as shown in

FIG 12

Figure 12. The thumb is on one side and the second and third fingers upon the opposite side. The little finger rests against the near end and the forefinger at the far end. Held thus the cards are kept perfectly together so that it is impossible to see how many there really are. You show that you have four aces. You draw off the top ace, the little finger moving away to permit this, and show it. You slide it back underneath the packet as you say : " The first ace."

You do the same with the second and third aces, showing them and putting them beneath the packet, but the fourth ace you replace on top of the packet after you have shown it. As a result of this manœuvre your packet of seven cards will be arranged, from the top, an ace, three indifferent cards, the other three aces.

Having shown the four aces you put them, very carefully and deliberately, on the top of the pack and say : " Now, no kidding this time," and you turn over the top card, an ace, and turn it face down again.

Then you deliberately deal the four top cards on to the carpet in a row from left to right and say : " Now on each ace I deal three more cards." Commencing with the left hand heap you do precisely what you say. As a result you will make four heaps. The left hand heap will consist of the four aces.

The other three heaps will consist of indifferent cards. The audience should believe that each heap consists of an ace surmounted by three ordinary cards.

In the trick we called " A Mathematical Certainty " (Part I) we gave you an example of the equivocal choice, and here we give you another. Your object is to have the left hand heap, consisting of the aces, " chosen " by one of the audience. You say to one of the ladies : " Would you mind choosing from these heaps either the inner or the outer pair." If she replies " the inner " you pick up that pair and drop them upon the pack, but if she replies " the outer " you say " Good," and push those two heaps forward a little, using only one finger to do so. *Then* you pick up the two inner packets and drop them upon the pack. Then you say to the lady: " Right or left please ? " and whichever she chooses you pick up the heap that does *not* contain the aces and drop it upon the pack, interpreting "right" to mean your own right and "left" to mean the lady's left. You leave no time for consideration of the point but at once ask the nearest spectator to draw his or her chair a little nearer and place one foot upon the remaining heap.

Now you approach your climax. You may say : " You have probably heard that a remarkable affinity exists between the four aces, which cannot bear to be separated. In the pack here we have three of the aces. Beneath this gentleman's foot we have the fourth ace, selected by chance, with three ordinary cards. In a moment the three aces will fly from the pack to join the fourth beneath the gentleman's foot. There ! " You run your thumb over the edge of the pack and then spread the cards face upwards in a long row upon the carpet. " The aces have gone ", you say, " and the three ordinary cards that were under your foot have flown under my coat." Here you reach under your coat and pull out the three cards you put into your lower vest pocket at the beginning of the trick.

And you conclude by asking the man to lift his foot and to turn up the four aces !

THE GLIDE FORCE

For the first time in this Handbook we mention the word " force " although the card " selected " in the trick called " The Forecast " was actually a " forced " card. There are various ways by which a conjurer may ensure that a certain card, predetermined, is " selected ", although the person who draws it deems that he has had a free choice. Then we say that the conjurer has " forced " the card. Needless to say we speak of this only amongst ourselves and never mention the word to the public.

The method used by the experts is called the " Classic Force " and we shall not describe it to you since it calls for more skill than you can easily acquire, more than we have undertaken to ask of you. For the moment we will show you how you can force a card by means of the Glide, which is very simple.

Put the card you desire to force upon the top of the pack and then shuffle it to the bottom. (All forces are stronger if they are preceded by a shuffle which gives the impression that you have no knowledge of the position of any of the cards in the pack.) Now hold the pack in the left hand in the position for the glide, draw back the bottom card, and begin to deal the cards slowly from the bottom, always dealing the second one, of course. Ask someone to call " stop " at any moment. At the request to stop, glide the bottom card back into position, and then draw it half way off the pack and permit the person who called to remove it, and place it in his pocket.

It is as simple as that !

THE FOUR ACES II

We shall now describe a trick with the four aces which is of such great simplicity that you may hesitate, perhaps, to believe that it really could be effective. But when your knowledge of conjuring has increased you will understand that it is often the simplest tricks that are the most mystifying. The simpler the solution the less likely it is that it will be considered.

We can remember, many years ago, seeing a well-known professional magician do this trick to a gathering of experts in the Magic Circle Club Room, and completely deceive all of them. And we can remember, also, their looks of blank astonishment when the simple secret was revealed to them.

The effect of the trick as it is remembered afterwards is that you shuffle a pack and place it upon the table. You ask someone to cut it into four approximately equal heaps. You turn over the cards on the top of the heaps and reveal the Four Aces.

The first thing to do is to get the four aces on the top of the pack and we will suggest a way in which you may do this without being suspected. First you glance at, and remember, the bottom card of the pack. Then you false shuffle to leave the card undisturbed, and you force it upon a spectator by means of the Glide Force which we have just described. You ask the spectator to put the card into his pocket without looking at it or letting anyone see what it is.

Now you ask the company if they think it is possible for you to discover the identity of the card that is missing from the pack by simply looking through it once only. The answer should be " No " because it is practically impossible to do this. You will have no difficulty, however, since you already know the card, having forced its selection. Let us suppose it was a six. Keeping the backs of the cards to the spectators you look through the pack and, every time you come to an ace you slip it to the top, while every time you come to a six you drop it, face down, upon the table. At the end you will have the four aces on the top of the pack and three sixes on the table. You turn the three sixes over and ask the spectator to remove the fourth one from his pocket. You gather up the four sixes and put them on the bottom of the pack.

Now you shuffle the pack, leaving the four aces undisturbed on the top, and put the cards down on the table. You ask a spectator to cut the pack into four approximately equal portions and, when he has done so, you look at them with a rather critical eye. It is impossible to give explicit instructions for the continuation of the trick because it depends so much upon how the cutting has been done, but you watch and note the position of the top portion of the pack which is capped by the four aces. We will call this heap A and the others B, C, and D. Perhaps C will be a little bigger than D. You say : " There are too many here " and you take two or three cards from C and put them on D. Then you seem to notice that B requires some cards and you take two (aces) from A and drop them on B. Then you take two more from A (aces again) and drop them on C. Then you observe that A is short and take a few cards from D to make it up. You also add a card from B (an ace). Then you take a few cards from C and put them on D, but decide that you have put too many and take one (an ace) back again. With that you appear to be satisfied.

You snap your fingers over the four heaps and then turn up the top cards, the Four Aces !

The movements we have given you are purely optional. You may use them if you wish or you may work out a series of movements for yourself, or you may improvise as the size of the heaps suggests to you. You have only to keep cool, take care to remember the position of the aces, and be careful not to overdo the thing and confuse yourself.

THE THIRTEEN PRINCIPLE

We stated above that it is practically impossible to discover the name of a card abstracted from the pack by merely looking through it once. We said " practically impossible " because we are not quite sure that it cannot be done by means of a mnemonic system and, in any case, we have seen so many fantastic things accomplished since we first dabbled in this conjuring business that we shall be reluctant always to use the word impossible without any qualification. But, it is not only possible but very simple to discover the card by going through the pack *twice*. Try it as you read our directions please.

Remove a card from your pack and place it aside, without looking at it please. Now go through the pack and add the " spot " values of the cards together, subtracting thirteen everytime your total exceeds that number, ignoring the Kings and counting the Queens as twelve spots and the Jacks as eleven spots. A simple example will show you that this is not so formidable a task as it may appear to be at first. I look through the pack that is beside my typewriter. The bottom card is the nine of Clubs, but I take no notice of the suits and simply think " nine." The next is the five of hearts. Nine and five are fourteen. I deduct thirteen and carry one. The next card is a seven which, added to one, makes eight. Another seven makes fifteen and again I deduct thirteen and carry two. The next card is a two (two and two are four) then comes a King, which I ignore, and a three (four and three are seven) followed by a Queen, which I count as twelve, taking my total to nineteen. I immediately deduct thirteen, reducing the total to six, to which I add the next card, a nine, making fifteen. I at once return to two by deducting thirteen, and I carry on in this way until I reach the end of the pack, when my final figure is eight. This is then subtracted from thirteen to give me the value of the missing card.

I look through the pack a second time for the fives and find the five of Clubs, five of Spades, and five of Diamonds, and I know that the abstracted card is the five of Hearts.

Do not think that you need to be a mathematical wizard to do this trick. It is very rarely that your figure goes over twenty and after a few trials you will find that the deduction of thirteen almost becomes automatic.

THE SLIP FORCE

Just as we gave you more than one way to control a selected card we think we should give you an alternative method of forcing a card. The Slip Force which we shall describe is easy to do and absolutely certain in its action. It is therefore very popular with amateur magicians, who generally do it very badly. We shall give you a method which is absolutely undetectable because the secret action is entirely covered by a natural movement.

You secretly place the card you desire to force upon the top of the pack and you false shuffle so as to leave the card there.

You state that you wish to have a card selected entirely by chance and that you will ask a lady to thrust the bottom card, face up, into the pack at any point she desires. You remove the bottom card as you speak and hand it, face up, to one of the ladies. You hold the pack in the palm of the left hand, face down, with the thumb across the back of the top card and the four fingers against its right side. and you ask the lady to thrust the corner of her card into the end of the pack wherever she desires. When she has done so you bring the right hand over the pack and grasp all the cards, above her face-up one, between the right third finger at the far end and the thumb at the near end, and you open the pack to the right at that point as if it were a book, the left thumb moving away to permit this, as shown in Figure 13. With the cards in this position

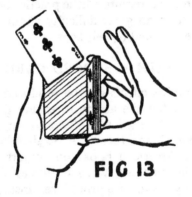

FIG 13

you will find that the tips of the left second and third fingers rest against the back of the top card of the pack (the force card). Please notice also that the right first and second fingers are unoccupied. Now you do several things at the same time and you must practise them so that you can do them without any excessive haste yet with all the actions blending together into one smooth motion. First you draw your hands back a little to free the pack from the face up card held by the lady. Then you press upon the top card with the left middle fingers and you turn the right hand a little towards yourself. The left fingers drag the top card off the upper packet as the right hand carries the latter away and the card is slipped, like a flash, upon the lower packet. The right hand, carrying the upper packet, moves in an arc to the face-up card the lady holds, grasps it between the unoccupied first and second fingers, and takes it from her. The left hand is immediately extended towards the lady with the lower packet as you say : " We will not use the card above, which we have all seen, but the one below." The lady accordingly takes the top card of lower packet.

The superiority of our method over those generally used and described lies in the action of taking the face up card from the lady with the hand that holds the top packet and thus giving us a natural reason for moving this hand away, a movement which entirely masks the slipping of the force card from the top to the centre.

The Slip Force will require a little practice before you can do it well but there is no great difficulty about it provided that your hands are reasonably well kept.

WITH A FORCED CARD

Many remarkable effects can be produced when you have learned to force, but the ability to ensure the selection of a certain card must be used with discretion and not abused. I think it was Mr. Jean Hugard, Australian-born author of a number of fine American books on conjuring, who first remarked that the amateur, when he forces a card, is apt to reveal the fact by his unwise procedure. Instead of continuing as he would have done with a freely selected card he hands the pack to the " selector " and tells him to replace the card himself and to shuffle the cards well. This, of course, is wrong. Proceed in your usual way. Have the card returned as you always do and shuffle the pack yourself. Afterwards, if you wish, you may hand the cards to a spectator for shuffling.

We will give you an excellent trick as an example of the way to use a forced card.

First you glance at the bottom card of the pack, remember its name, and shuffle it to the top. Let us suppose that this card is the ace of Diamonds. Force this ace upon one of the spectators by means of either of the methods we have taught you. Ask the selector to show the card to the company and then let him replace it in the pack. Shuffle the pack well and then, as if it were an afterthought, ask him if he would like to shuffle also. When he has shuffled take the pack from him and say : " I want to find the Joker. I suppose, by the way, it was not the Joker you chose ? No ! Good." You fan the pack between your hands and you find, first the forced card (the ace of Diamonds) and then the Joker. You remove the Joker and throw it down upon the table. Then you cut the pack to take the ace to the top and you immediately shuffle the pack again, this time shuffling the ace to the bottom. You put the pack down on the table by the side of the Joker.

Now you ask the selector of the card to cut the pack, and by a gesture you indicate that you wish him to put the part cut down beside the other half. You drop the Joker face up upon the original top portion of the pack and you complete the cut by picking up the bottom half and dropping it on top of the Joker.

Now you remind the audience of the course of events. A card has been selected and replaced in the pack which has been shuffled by the selector. The position of the card in the pack is therefore entirely a matter of chance. The selector has cut the pack and the cut has been marked by the Joker. " There are some things that can only be described as remarkable coincidences until they happen again and again . . . and then one calls them magic." As you say the last words you take hold of the Joker and with it turn over the top half of the pack to reveal the selected card.

The recapitulation of events in this case has served two purposes. It has " built up " the effect and it has allowed an interval to elapse between the cutting of the pack and the ultimate disclosure of the result, an interval which has given time for the details of the somewhat irregular cutting procedure to have faded from the spectators' minds.

THE CARD UNDER THE CARPET

But it is when we use an extra card, a duplicate card, that the force really comes into its own and, by its means, a selected card is apparently made to fly from the pack and reappear elsewhere. Sometimes two or three cards are forced and made to reappear in some piece of apparatus. Actually, of course, it is the duplicates that reappear. We are not including tricks with apparatus in this Handbook but we will briefly mention some of the best things of this sort, which may be purchased from dealers in magical equipment.

There are various kinds of frames which may be shown empty and will yet " produce " selected cards. In our companion volume *A Handbook of Conjuring* you will find the description of a trick with a small picture frame and a number of postcards which may also be done with a playing card. There is a special sword which, when plunged into a pack of cards which has been thrown into the air, will produce a duplicate of the chosen card, impaled upon its point. Truly an astonishing effect. There are various forms of the Rising Card Trick also, in which selected cards rise out of the pack while it stands in a glass or in a simple piece of apparatus.

For the amateur performer the trick we shall now describe is, in many ways, equal to any of these apparatus tricks and has the advantage over all of them that it needs no expensive equipment. You will need only an extra card taken from another pack having the same patterned back. (When you buy your cards, always buy two packs at a time, so that you will have plenty of different duplicate cards available. There is an old story told amongst conjurers of a professional appearing at a theatre who had the nine of clubs "chosen" from the pack twice nightly all the week !)

You will also need momentary access, alone, to the room in which you will be performing, some time beforehand, so that you may slip your duplicate card under the corner of the carpet, or under a rug, at the part of the room which you will occupy when you do your turn.

Now, in the course of your performance you look through

the pack and locate the duplicate of the card under the carpet. You cut the pack to bring this card to the top and you remove the Joker as the ostensible reason for looking through the pack. You hand the Joker to one of the spectators and invite him to thrust the corner of it into the pack. You use the slip force to have your duplicated card selected. You allow a second spectator to select a card in exactly the same way, by thrusting the Joker into the pack, but this time you do not slip the top card. You allow a real choice to be made. However you must proceed in *exactly* the same way as you did when you forced the card.

Now you have the two cards replaced in the pack and you bring them both to the top by one of the methods previously described, and you false shuffle to leave the cards there. The duplicate of the card under the carpet should be the second card from the top of the pack.

You go down on one knee and put the pack down on the carpet near to the spot beneath which the concealed card lies. You ask the person who drew the freely chosen card to name it, and you pick up the pack and throw it down upon the carpet so that the card he names appears face up on top of it. (See the trick called " The Revolution " which we described in connection with " Think of a Number " in Part I.)

You turn this card face down again and ask the other selector to name his card, the forced one. Once more you pick up the pack and slap it down upon the carpet, but, as you do not slide the top card off the pack, nothing happens. At this you must appear to be very surprised. You pick up the pack and slap it down again, still without result. You turn the pack towards yourself and, frowning furiously, you look through it as though you were seeking the card. Suddenly you smile and say " Ah ! I must have slapped it down too hard ", and you turn back the carpet to reveal the chosen card !

THE ONE WAY PACK

We now introduce you to another principle which has almost unlimited possibilities if it is used with imagination.

If you will examine a pack of cards of the kind which has a geometrical pattern, or a " wall-paper " pattern to its back, you will observe at first sight that the pattern is the same whichever way the card is turned. We will now ask you to examine the cards more carefully, comparing one with another and we shall be very surprised if, after close inspection, you do not find some slight difference in the patterns at the two ends of the pack. The difference, no doubt, will be very small, such as a leaf with a sharp point at one end and one with a round point at the other, or a trifling difference in the position of two dots, but, nevertheless, the difference will be easy to discern when you know what to look for, and it will be repeated in every card of the pack. Some excellent cards may be found for this purpose which have a check design of small squares, in which the corner square at one end is white while that at the opposite end is red or blue, according to the pack.

Now, if you arrange the cards so that they all point the same way, that is to say so that all the pointed leaves or all the white corner squares are at the same end, you have a " one way pack." Take any card from this pack and turn it round and, however much the pack is shuffled you can always find that card by looking at the backs.

The brightly coloured bridge cards, so popular today, which bear on their backs pictures of kittens, pretty girls, or Swiss mountains, according to taste, are all " one way packs " but cannot be used for our purpose because they are so *too obviously*. We can introduce another stratagem, however, in order to use them. First you mix all the cards so that some of the kittens for example, are head ups and others are tails up, and then you make a minute mark in one corner of each card. You will now have a one way pack which is independent of the back design, and you will always be able to find a card that has been reversed in this pack by the position of your mark. The marks may be made with coloured ink to match the colour of the cards or may be simple pencil dots ; or you may remove a tiny fragment of coloured surface, with the point of a sharp knife, to leave a white spot on the card.

We will give you two or three tricks to illustrate the use of this principle.

ONE WAY ELIMINATION

Using a one way pack, all the cards of which are pointing in the same direction, you spread it between your hands for a card to be selected. When the card has been taken you close the pack and hold it in your left hand while you ask the chooser to show his choice to the rest of the company. You watch carefully to see how he handles the card and if he turns it end for end. If he does not turn the card round you take the pack in your right hand, grasping it by the far end, and spread it in a fan with a twist of the fingers, asking him to replace the card. Thus you have reversed the pack and his card will be pointing in a different direction from all the others. On the other hand, if you see him turn his card, you fan the pack in your left hand without reversing it.

You may now shuffle the pack and let the selector shuffle also, after which you divide the pack into two heaps and invite him to guess which one contains his card. You take the heap he indicates and fan it between your hands, showing him the faces and looking at the backs yourself. You look for the reversed card, of course. If you do not find it you say, " I think you guessed wrong that time " and discard the heap, but if you do find it you congratulate him upon having guessed correctly.

Now you give the half pack a shuffle and divide it into two portions again, asking him to guess once more which packet contains his card. Again you fan the cards of the packet he chooses, congratulate him if he is correct, and discard the packet that does not contain the card.

The twelve or so cards that remain you shuffle and divide into two portions. Holding one lot in each hand you spread them so that you can see the backs sufficiently well to distinguish the reversed card, and you ask the assisting spectator to guess " left or right." Again you tell him if he is right or wrong and you discard the " wrong " cards.

You continue thus until you have only one card left, which proves to be the selected one.

THE TRANSPOSED CARD

With all the cards of your one way pack pointing in the same direction, you shuffle it well and put it down upon the table. Now you cut the pack into two portions which you place one on either side of the table. To do this you grasp the pack by its ends between the second fingers and thumbs of each hand, the left hand grasping the bottom half and the right hand the top half of the pack. You separate the hands, each holding half the pack, and put the halves down on opposite sides of the table. You will find that this naturally leaves the one way backs of the two halves pointing in opposite directions.

You retire from the table and invite a spectator to remove a card from one of the heaps, to show it to the company, and to put it within the other heap. Then you ask him to shuffle both the heaps and replace them on the table.

Now you return to the table and reassemble the pack. In doing so you reverse the movements you made when you cut the pack. That is to say, you grasp each heap by its end, bring them in front of you, and place one on top of the other. All the cards will now be pointing in the same direction except the transposed card.

There are many ways in which you might complete the trick but we will suggest that you use the following. Take the cards and begin to look through them, searching for the reversed back. Cut the pack anywhere and remove the top card. Look at this card and name it, saying, for example, " Was the selected card the ten of Clubs ? " On receiving the negative response drop the card on to the table, allowing the spectators to get a fleeting glimpse of its face, so that they may see that it is, indeed, the card you named ; but do not deliberately show it to them.

Now find the reversed card and cut that to the top. Look at the card which, for convenience of description, we will suppose is the Queen of Spades, and say " Was the selected card the nine of Diamonds ? " Drop the card on to the table on the right hand side of the first one, but do not allow the face of the card to be seen. You must remember the name by which you miscalled this card.

Cut the pack a third time and take the new top card. Look at it and name it, saying, for example, " Was it the two of Clubs ? " Again drop the card upon the table, to the right of the last one, without letting its face be seen.

Say, " Three attempts and three failures. It is not the . . . . " pick up the left hand card and glance at his face, then replace it without showing it and continue your sentence . . . . " the ten of Clubs or . . . . " look at the centre card, again, needless to say, without showing it . . . . " the nine of Diamonds " (miscalling it again) " or . . . . " look at the right hand card, this time tilting it a little so that its face may be seen and naming it . . . . " the two of Clubs ? Too bad ! "

Ask a lady to choose one of the three cards and, by means of the equivocal force with which you should now be familiar, interpret her selection to mean the centre card and replace the other two in the pack. Now announce that you will make the previously selected card change places with the one the lady has now chosen. Ask for the name of the selected card. Command the cards to change places. Make a crackling noise with your thumb against the edge of the pack and ask someone to turn up the card upon the table . . . . and there is the selected card, the Queen of Spades !

You have there a fine example of the real art of conjuring, an art in which acting is of far more importance than dexterity.

IN YOUR HANDS

You secretly reverse the top half of your one way pack, which you put down upon the table. You cut the pack, cutting only about a quarter of the cards, and you complete the cut. The result of these actions is that the centre of the pack points in the opposite direction to the rest of the cards.

You invite a spectator to take the pack in his own hands while you retire to the side of the room. You request him to take a card from the centre of the pack, to show it to the company, to replace it on the top of the pack, to cut the pack and complete the cut, and, finally, to replace the cards upon the table.

The selected card will now be in the centre of the pack pointing in the opposite direction to all its neighbours.

Spread the cards in a face up over-lapping row upon the table and ask one of the spectators to indicate which portion of the pack contains the card. Remove about a dozen cards from the point indicated and spread them in a fan, holding it with the backs of the cards towards yourself. You will be able to see the position of the selected card quite easily because of its reversed back.

Ask the selector to concentrate his mind upon his card. Run your finger backwards and forwards along the top of the fan once or twice and then stop at the selected card, draw it from the fan, and hand it to him.

THE FIVE CARD TRICK

This is, in the Author's personal opinion, the best trick that can be done with a one way pack.

You begin by giving the pack to be shuffled and, when you receive it back, you ask a spectator to thrust a pencil into the centre of the pack and push out a small packet of cards. You pull these cards out and drop them on the top of the pack. Then you take the top five cards in your right hand and spread them into a fan, which you show to one of the spectators, asking him to think of one of them. You hand him also a slip of paper and a pencil and ask him to write the name of his card upon it, to fold it, and to hand it to another spectator. You turn away while he writes so that it is impossible for you to see. You ask the second spectator to look at the name of the card upon the paper and then to mentally select a second one from the five that you hold. You ask him to write the name of his card on the slip of paper for the sake of the record. Throughout these proceedings you take care to hold the five cards so that the spectators can see that you do not look at the faces of them.

Now you replace the five cards in different parts of the pack, quite naturally *reversing them*, and you hand the pack to someone to shuffle.

When you receive the pack back you take a small number of cards from the top, six, seven, or eight, and spread them in a fan. You watch for a reversed card amongst them. You show these cards to each of the assisting spectators asking if the cards of which they thought are amongst them. Should they both say " No " you put these cards aside and take another small batch. You keep watch for the cards that are reversed in the pack and take care never to include more than one such card in any fan. So, when either of the choosers tells you that his card is amongst those you hold you know at once that it is the reversed one. After some hesitation, acting as though you were " mind reading " you pick out the correct card from the fan. You carry on thus to find the second selected card.

THE PACK REVEALS IT

We shall now leave the One Way Pack to give you severa tricks which depend upon a pre-arrangement of the cards. Some astonishing effects may be produced by this means.

You arrange your pack so that the top card is a ten, the second a nine, the third an eight, and so on down to the tenth card, which will be an ace. The suits do not matter, it is only the numerical sequence 10, 9, 8, 7, 6, 5, 4, 3, 2, 1 which is required. Make a little bend or crimp in one corner of the Ace so that you will be able to cut at that card (see " The Corner Crimp " in Part I).

False shuffle the pack to leave the top stock (your ten arranged cards) undisturbed, and then invite one of the company to select a card and to show it to the others. Cut at the crimp for the replacement of the selected card, drop the cut back on top of it, and then false shuffle again, leaving the top eleven cards undisturbed.

Now spread the pack upon the table so that the top twelve or fifteen cards lie in an overlapping line, and ask one of the company to touch any one of the cards thus exposed. Turn up the card that is touched and call the number of spots upon it. Count that number of cards along the row and turn up the next one . . . . the selected card.

ODD AND EVEN

We have previously shown you how you may arrange a few cards in the course of one trick for the purpose of another, and we shall now give you a trick in which, with colossal audacity, the conjurer arranges the whole pack in front of his audience. But it will be, of course, quite a simple arrangement.

The effect of the trick is similar to that of " The Transposed Card " which we described when we were discussing the One Way Pack, but the present trick may be performed with any cards. First you hand the pack to a spectator for thorough shuffling and, when you receive it back, you cut it into two equal portions. You invite a spectator, while you turn away, to take any card from either heap, show it to the company, and bury it in the other heap. You then direct him to reassemble the pack by placing the two heaps together, to cut and to complete the cut.

This having been done you take the pack and look through it very carefully, You appear to make some mental calculation and then you remove one card and put it face down upon the table. You ask the name of the transposed card and then you turn over the card on the table. You have failed !

" I can't understand this," you say. " Will you try again ? " Once more you cut the pack into two halves. You turn away while the spectator takes any card from either heap and buries it in the other. He reassembles the pack, cuts, and completes the cut. All this while you stand with your back to the table. You turn now and look through the pack and, after a little hesitation, you remove one card and put it down upon the table. You ask the name of the transposed card and you turn over the one on the table. You are right !

With the knowledge of conjuring which you have gained from this Handbook you will be rather suspicious of that preliminary failure. In fact it is the secret of the trick. The first time you look through the pack you separate the cards between the odd ones and the even ones. As you pass the cards from the left hand into the right hand you put all the even cards in front and all the odd ones behind. (The odd cards, of course, are the Ace, three, five, seven, nine, Jack, and King . . . . the others are the even ones.) When you have the pack thus divided, you crimp the corner of the even card on the face of the pack, the bottom card, and then run through once more until you come to the first odd card. You throw this card down upon the table and then cut at the dividing point between odd and even, thus taking the crimped card to the centre.

Now, when you " try again ", you simply cut the pack at the crimped card and thus divide it into two approximately equal parts, one containing all the odd and the other all the even cards. You will now have no difficulty in finding the transposed card, one even card amongst all the odd ones or one odd card amongst the even ones.

Bear in mind that there is always a *possibility* that you may pick the correct card at the first attempt. In such a case conceal your own astonishment and take credit for the miracle you have performed . . . . with all due modesty, of course !

WITH TWO PACKS

One of the two packs which you will use for this experiment must be previously arranged so that the spot values of any two consecutive cards, when added together, will total either fourteen or fifteen. You will have to discard two aces to do this, so that the pack will consist of only fifty cards. The

following is an example of how the beginning of the pack
might run :

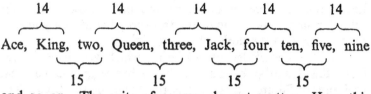

and so on. The suits of course, do not matter. Have this
pack in your pocket, in its case, and commence the trick with
the other one, which is without any arrangement.

You first shuffle the pack and then you spread it between
your hands and ask someone to select a card. As you pass the
cards from hand to hand you secretly count them, and you
keep a break beneath the fourteenth one. When a card has
been selected you close the pack and slip the tip of your little
finger into the break to hold the division beneath the fourteenth
card. You ask the chooser to show his card to the company
and then you cut at the break for him to return it to the pack.
You drop the cut back on top of his card, deliberately square
up the pack, and execute your top stock shuffle. The selected
card will be the fifteenth in the pack. You hand this pack to
a spectator to hold, first, as a wise precaution, putting an
elastic band around it in case he should be seized with a sudden
urge to shuffle. Always be careful in such cases, particularly
with habitual card players, many of whom automatically
shuffle a pack when it is handed to them.

You now produce the second pack, which you remove
from its case and casually cut once or twice. This cutting does
not spoil the order of the cards. A pack of cards that has been
arranged in sequence is very much like one of those lines of
marching caterpillars of which one occasionally reads. Divert
the leader from his course so that he veers round the trunk of
a tree and begins to follow the last in line and all the caterpillars will march endlessly round and round the tree until
exhaustion overcomes them or you divert them once again.
It is thus with the arranged pack. The top card is always
ready to follow the bottom one and both of them are prepared

to become middle units. Cutting the pack, so long as the cut is properly completed, only creates new top and bottom cards, new first and last caterpillars, without altering the sequence of the units of the pack. But to return to our trick.

Hand the pack to another spectator and ask him to cut it wherever he wishes and to remove two cards. Take the pack from him and ask him to add together the spot value of the two cards he has removed, explaining that Jacks count as eleven, Queens as twelve, and Kings as thirteen. Ask him then to announce the answer to his piece of arithmetic which, because of the arrangement of the cards, is bound to be either fourteen or fifteen.

Turn to the spectator who holds the other pack and ask him, if the number is fourteen, to deal fourteen cards from his pack and to place the fifteenth in his pocket. If, however, the number is fifteen, ask him to count down in the pack and to put the fifteenth card in his pocket.

Pause now for your necessary recapitulation which will build up the effect, which is truly astonishing. One person has selected a card which has been shuffled back into the pack. A second person has taken two cards at random from another pack and added their values together to produce an haphazard figure. A third person has put into his pocket the card standing at that number in the shuffled pack.

Quietly ask the name of the selected card and then request the spectator to remove it from his pocket.

EIGHT KINGS

There are various ways in which a pack may be arranged so that the conjurer can remember the complete order of the cards, from the first to last, and so that the sight of one card will tell him the name of the next. This leads to a host of interesting possibilities which we can only touch in passing in the course of this Handbook.

One of the oldest and simplest ideas is that known as the

" Eight Kings " because the order of the cards is remembered by means of the following jingle :—

> Eight Kings threatened to save
> Ninety-five ladies for one sick Knave.

These cryptic lines are easily remembered and will recall to you the order of eight, King, three, ten, two, seven (save), nine, five, Queen, four, Ace (one), six, Jack (knave).

You must now fix upon an arrangement of suits. You may take the Bridge order, Clubs, Diamonds, Hearts, Spades, or one of alternating colours, such as Clubs, Hearts, Spades, Diamonds, which can be remembered by another ancient formula, CHaSeD, in which the capitals give the suits. Let us suppose you decide upon the latter.

To arrange your pack you first sort it out into the four suits. Now take one of the Clubs, let us suppose it is the six. You remember your lines about the sick Knave and you place on the face up *six* of Clubs the *knave* of Hearts. You return to the commencement of your memorized lines and you find the *eight* of Spades, then the *King* of Diamonds, the *three* of Clubs, the *ten* of Hearts, the *two* of Spades, the *seven* of Diamonds, and you carry on in this way until you reach the last card of the pack, which will be the Ace of Diamonds. If you wish to include the Joker in the pack you may do so provided you take care to remember at exactly what point in the arrangement you have placed it. It is advisable always to have it at the same point.

Naturally, with the pack arranged thus, you can always tell what card has been taken from it by looking at the one that was above it. The best way to do this is to cut the pack at the point from which the card is drawn and then to secretly glance at the bottom card. Then if, when the card is replaced, you undercut the pack, that is, draw off the bottom half and have the chosen card replaced beneath it, you will restore the pack to the complete arrangement. A better use for the arranged pack is given in the trick that follows.

THREE CARD DIVINATION

With your cards arranged in the Eight Kings order you invite three spectators each to choose one from the pack, which you spread between your hands in the usual fashion. As each person selects his card you open the pack a little to allow him to withdraw it and then, with your left thumb, you pull the card which was beneath the chosen one about an inch to the left. You press down a little on the edge of this card and tilt it up with your thumb so that you can slide the top portion of the pack beneath it as you close the cards. The card next in sequence to the chosen one thus becomes the top card of the pack. You do this each time a card is selected so that, at the conclusion, you have three cards on the top of the pack which follow, in the Eight Kings order, the cards which have been selected. As each card is drawn you ask the choosers to put them into their pockets without looking at them, " so that there can be no question of thought reading being the simple solution to the problem in progress."

When you have slipped the three cards to the top of the pack you false shuffle by simply drawing off the three cards, one by one, and then shuffling the rest of the pack on top of them.

You are now able to " divine " the name of the three cards in the spectators pockets, " three cards which nobody knows." You fan the cards towards yourself and pretend to study them. Naturally you have only to look at the bottom card of the pack and go one backwards in your arrangement to know the name of the first selected card. For example, if the bottom card is the five of Diamonds .... you know that a nine always precedes a five and a spade a diamond. Then the first selected card is the nine of spades. Simply ask the spectator to put his hand into his pocket and hand you the nine of Spades !

In exactly the same way the second card from the bottom will give you the second selected card and the third from the bottom the last selected one.

SI STEBBINS' ARRANGEMENT

Another method of arranging a pack, of American origin, is known by the name of its inventor, Si Stebbins, and is, perhaps, superior to the Eight Kings arrangement. It is very simple and may be summed up in the words " change the suit and add three." Thus, supposing you are using the Bridge order of the suits and you begin your arrangement with the Ace of Clubs, you would follow that card with the four of Diamonds, seven of Hearts, ten of Spades, King of Clubs, three of Diamonds, six of Hearts, and so on, always adding three points to the last card and changing the suit. Your pack which started with the Ace of Clubs would finish with the Jack of Spades.

All the tricks done with the Eight Kings arrangement may be performed with the Si Stebbins' pack and to them we would add the following excellent trick which makes use of the fact that, in this arrangement, the cards of each suit run in descending order, that is to say, the King of Clubs is followed four cards later by the Queen, and four cards later still by the Jack of Clubs, and so on down to the Ace. And this is so for all the suits.

ONE IN FIVE

You seat a spectator at the table and place the pack, arranged in Si Stebbins' order, in front of him. You turn your back and instruct him to cut the pack anywhere he wishes and to complete the cut. You ask him if he is satisfied that the cut was made at random or if he would wish to cut again. You make sure that he is satisfied that he has had a free choice. You ask him then to look at the card he cut, the new top card of the pack, to show it to the company, and to put it face down upon the table. You then ask him to deal four more cards on to the table and to put the pack into his pocket. Finally you ask him to mix up the five cards on the table and then to arrange them in one row.

You turn back to the table and examine the cards one after

the other. Finally you pick up one of the cards and hand it to the assisting spectator. It is the chosen card.

If you will go over the action of the trick again, bearing in mind the manner in which the pack is arranged you will understand that of the five cards on the table two will be of the same suit and the others of the three other suits. The selected card will always be the higher of the two cards of the same suit.

READING THE PACK

The ancient trick of reading all the cards of the pack without seeing their faces may be done, of course, with the arranged pack, although it would be unwise to read too many cards because of the risk that the regular rotation of the suits might be noticed by an observant spectator. However, by the use of a little ingenuity an excellent trick can be made of this feat which can well follow some other effect with an arranged pack.

A little preparation will be necessary. Pinned to the back of your trousers, underneath your coat, you must have a little spring paper clip. In your right hand upper-most vest pocket you have six cards taken from another pack with the same back design. You must remember the names of these six cards and their order. If you always use the same six cards for this trick their names will soon be familiar to you.

First you false shuffle the pack by the method we described in Part I under the heading of " False Shuffling IV ", leaving a good stock undisturbed on the top of the pack after you have cut it. You hold the pack behind your back with both hands while you tell your story of the possibility of card reading by sightless vision. While you are talking you must do several things and you should therefore take the pains to determine beforehand exactly what you will say, so that you will be able to talk without hesitation while you are thinking of something else. The first thing you do is to put five cards in the clip under the back of your coat. You keep your arms pressed closely to your sides while you do this and use only your hands and wrists so that no movement of your elbows will be seen to warn the spectators that you are busily at work. Next you palm the top card of the pack in your right hand and you take in the same hand the bottom card which you bring forward as you say, " Notice please that I do not hold the card up like this and then name it. I name the cards while they are still behind my back and normal vision of any sort is quite impossible."

You replace the card on the bottom of the pack behind your back but, just as the hand retires with the card, you glance at the palmed one and, from it, you at once know the names of the five cards in the clip and the cards that are on the top of the pack. You put the palmed card on the bottom of the pack also, as by omitting to read this card you break the sequence of the cards you do read, naming two small batches instead of one long series.

You now name the top card of the pack (it follows the palmed one in the arrangement) and bring it forward and drop it upon the table. You may then read three more cards from the top, fairly rapidly, in the same way. For example, supposing that you are using the Si Stebbins' arrangement, if the palmed card was the King of Clubs the cards read will be the three of Diamonds, six of Hearts, nine of Spades, and Queen of Clubs.

At this point you bring the pack forward again and hand it to someone to shuffle. On receiving it back you put it behind your back again and quickly pull the five cards from the clip and add them to the top of the pack. Now you must think backwards from the King of Clubs . . . . ten of Spades, seven of Hearts, four of Diamonds, Ace of Clubs, Jack of Spades . . . . and you are ready to call the names of the five cards, beginning with the top one, the Jack of Spades. If you think it desirable you may produce the cards in an irregular order. You call the first two cards as you stand facing the spectators with the cards behind you. Then turn sideways to them and turn up the next three cards as you name them.

Again hand the pack to someone to shuffle and remark that some people sometimes think that it is not really a question of sightless vision but of a superior sense of touch. Take the pack back and drop it into your coat pocket as you say that you will name the cards without either seeing or touching them. Name the first of the six cards in your upper vest pocket. Thrust your hand into your coat pocket and apparently bring out from it the card you have named but really take the card from the upper vest pocket. (You will remember that we used this idea also in the trick called " Thought Divined " in Part I). Name the second card of your memorized six and remove it in the same way. Then name the remaining four cards one after the other and remove them very rapidly from the pocket, bringing the trick to a brisk termination.

PREPARED CARDS

There are so many different kinds of special cards and prepared packs which may be made, or may be purchased from the dealers in conjuring apparatus, that it is quite impossible to deal with them adequately in the space at our disposal and, in any case, we strongly advise you to use none of them until, at least, your experience of conjuring is sufficient to enable you to make a sound judgment of the merits and demerits of each one of them. You will also find that in your early conjuring years your chief opportunities to perform will be found in the homes of your friends, perhaps after a game of cards, and you will naturally use the cards that you find there rather than produce a pack of your own.

One of the oldest ideas in connection with special cards is to have in the pack one card which is a fraction longer or wider than all the others. Many makers of playing cards enclose in the outer wrapping of their packs a specimen card, either a blank card, an extra joker, or a bridge score card. These specimens often differ in size very slightly from the cards they accompany and will make excellent long or wide cards. Such a card can always be found in the shuffled pack by the feel of the fingers and can be used as a key card. If a selected card is replaced under the wide or long card, cutting he pack at that point will take the chosen card to the top.

A later and better idea is the short or narrow card made by taking a minute shaving from the end or side of a card. The short or narrow card is better than the long one because it cannot be accidentally discovered by a spectator who handles the pack. To find the short card you take the pack in the left hand and place the right hand fingers on the far end and the thumb upon the near end. Now you run the finger tips across the ends of the cards, raising them a little and releasing them one by one in a steady stream, when a slight pause in the even falling of the cards will tell you when you have reached the short one. A little practice will enable you to stop with accuracy at the short card. A narrow card is found in a similar way by running the thumb across the side of the pack.

Another idea, now fallen somewhat into disuse in this country but still popular with continental conjurers, is the bisauté pack which our American friends call the " stripper deck." The sides of this pack are trimmed to make all the cards very slightly wedge shaped, slightly wider at one end than at the other. When all the cards are arranged so that the wide ends are together the pack appears to be unprepared yet, if any card is reversed in the pack, that is to say, turned end for end, it can readily be found since it becomes a " wide " card at the narrow end of the pack. By holding the pack by the sides at one end, and running the fingers of the other hand down its long edges, a reversed card may be drawn out of the pack. Any number of cards reversed in this way may be drawn out thus with one action and put either on the top or the bottom of the pack, and it is this stripping of the cards from the pack which has suggested its American name, the stripper deck. (Various old English words like " deck " now no longer used in English have survived in the American language.) The bisauté pack is used in very much the same way as the One Way Pack, being turned round after the cards have been selected so that they will be replaced in reversed position. Most of the conjuring dealers who sell the stripper deck include with it very full instructions.

There are various ways in which the cards may be marked

so that they can be identified as readily from their backs as from their faces. Marked cards, or " reader decks " as the Americans call them, may be purchased ready made, or you may make your own. Red backed cards will be marked with red ink, and blue backed ones with blue ink, so that the markings will be practically invisible to anyone who does not know what to look for and where to look. The backs of most cards show a pattern in white upon a blue or red back-ground. The pattern generally consists of leaves, scrolls, dots, or points, all of which may be shortened, altered, or obliterated by a pen stroke. One of the best methods of marking consists in deciding upon twelve such points and to alter or erase the point that gives the value of the card. That is to say the seventh point will be altered on all the four sevens and the twelfth point on all the four Queens, while the kings will be left unmarked. Three further points will be required to give the suits, the clubs, diamonds, and hearts being marked while the spades are left untouched. So the only unmarked card in the pack will be the King of Spades. The cards can also be marked in this way by being pricked with a needle, in which case they are " read " by feeling with the finger tips, as a blind man reads braille. This is not an accomplishment you will learn in a few hours. Needless to say in all systems of marking the cards are marked at both ends.

A very good trick pack would be one consisting of marked cards arranged in Si Stebbins' order. When a card is drawn from this pack a glance at the back one of its former neighbours will give the name of the card withdrawn.

Various trick packs are sold, made with long and short cards, cards stuck together in pairs, cards with false indices, cards that are all alike, double backed cards, double faced cards, and an infinity of ingenious ideas. We advise you to have nothing to do with any of them. Most of them have been invented for only one purpose, to sell to uninformed amateurs and clumsy dabblers in conjuring.

There are also some ingenious mechanical changing cards which, if intelligently used, can find a place in a conjuring programme, such as the beautifully made "moving pip cards" which can change from, say, fives to sevens. By simply moving a tiny lever you may make two pips detach themselves from the others and move to occupy the vacant spaces on the card.

Occasionally the playing card manufacturers, prompted by the more ingenious and irresponsible members of the fraternity, give us some excellent joke cards which are worth collecting and using occasionally. Imagine the feelings of a spectator who finds that he has "chosen" from the pack the fifteen of Diamonds or the seven and a half of Clubs !

IN CONCLUSION

We should not be doing our duty to the reader if we left him without a few words of general advice and counsel. It would have been better, perhaps, to have done this at the beginning rather than at the end of our Handbook, but we know well that Prefaces are never read, and hungry diners seldom pause to read articles on dietetics.

You may have discovered already, by grim experience, that all conjuring tricks, even the most simple, require a certain amount of practice before they can be done with any success. If they are to be done really well they need a considerable amount of practice. The chief thing is to moderate your enthusiasm and not rush off to show your new tricks to the neighbours before you have learned them thoroughly. And to learn a trick thoroughly it is best to proceed by regular and well defined stages.

First, read our description of the trick at least twice and make sure that you follow our explanation and understand exactly what you must do and precisely what the effect of the trick will be to the spectators. Next make sure that you can do, *with ease*, all the manipulations which the trick requires. If, for example, you have to false shuffle the pack, you must practise this shuffle until you can do it without thinking about it, just as when you shuffle the cards fairly. If, after that, you have to palm a card, you must also practise your palming until you can do it as easily as you can sign your name.

Having made sure that all the different secret actions are well within your ability to do, you can begin to perform the trick *to yourself*, as a whole, first with the book in front of you and then from memory. After doing it half a dozen times you should be ready to advance another step.

Sit down in an armchair and spend half an hour thinking about the trick and considering what you will say when you are doing it. We have given you numerous lines in the Handbook which may serve as examples of the kind of talk you need, but we have refrained, deliberately, from giving you too much talk because it is essential that what you say should come naturally from you, and should suit your character and personality. Make a few notes of suitable " lines of patter ", including any jokes that may occur to you as apt and suitable, but do not upset yourself by racking your brains for witticisms. A conjurer does not have to be a comedian.

You will now be able to REHEARSE your trick, combining words and actions, and going through it several times. Stand before your wardrobe mirror and do the trick to yourself a number of times, watching the expression of your face and checking generally on your acting of the little play, for every conjuring trick is a play in miniature. In this rehearsal you must talk *out loud* as if you were actually doing the trick to a company of spectators. It is not sufficient to simply mutter the words to yourself. The rehearsal must be a real attempt to perform the trick exactly as you will perform it, soon, to a " real live audience."

We have said that a trick is a miniature play and, if it is to be a successful play, it must be acted with conviction. When you order a card to fly from the centre of the pack to the top you must express your command as though you were convinced of its necessity and sure of its efficacy. It is only by adequately rehearsing your words and actions that you will be able to do this.

When you have conscientiously rehearsed you may face

your audience with confidence and assurance. You will probably feel rather nervous but your nervousness will not effect your ability. We hope indeed, that you will feel nervous, for it is always a sign of the artist to be a little highly strung, and unless you have something of the artist in you, you will never make a good conjurer.

BIBLIOGRAPHY

SELECTED AND ADVANCED WORKS

Erdnase, S. W. *The Expert at the Card Table.* Chas. T. Powner Co., Chicago, 1944.*

Hilliard, J. N. *Card Magic.* (forms part of separate book, *Greater Magic.*) C. W. Jones, Minneapolis, Minn., 1945.

Hugard, J., ed. *Encyclopedia of Card Tricks.* Max Holden, New York City, 1937.*

Hugard, J. and Fred Braue. *Expert Card Technique.* G. Starke, New York City, 1950.*

Hugard, J. and Fred Braue. *The Royal Road to Card Magic.* Harper and Bros., New York-London, 1948.*

Young, M. N. *Hobby Magic.* Trilon Press, Div. of Magazine & Periodical Pntg. & Pub. Co., Inc., Brooklyn, N. Y., 1950.

* Available in reprint editions by Dover Publications, Inc.

INDEX